TURN[...]

the

HEAR[...]

to

GOD

by St. Theophan the Recluse

Translated by Igumen Iona Zhiltsov
and Father Ken Kaisch

CONCILIAR PRESS
Ben Lomond, California

Turning the Heart to God

Published by
>Conciliar Press
P.O. Box 76
Ben Lomond, California 95005-0076

Printed in Canada

ISBN 1-888212-22-5

Library of Congress Cataloguing-in-Publication Data

Feofan, Saint, Bishop of Tambov and Shatsk, 1815–1894.
    [O pokaianii. English]
    Turning the heart to God / by St. Theophan the Recluse ;
    translated by Iona Zhiltsov and Ken Kaish.
        p. cm.
    Includes bibliographical references and index.
    ISBN 1-888212-22-5
    1. Christian life—Orthodox Eastern authors.
    2. Repentance—Orthodox Eastern Church.
I. Zhiltsov, Iona, 1962– II. Kaisch, Ken, 1948– III. Title.

BX382.F466 2001
248.4'819—dc21   00-065728

For Marleen,
in thanksgiving for her friendship and encouragement

Table of Contents

Acknowledgments

All books are cooperative endeavors, and this book is no exception. First and foremost, we want to acknowledge the good efforts of Suzanne Kaisch, who opened her home and her hospitality to Igumen Iona during his stay in the U.S. She was an unfailingly gracious hostess who took the special needs of Igumen Iona to heart. In addition, she was Fr. Ken's patient editor and corrected many of his mistakes.

There are many others who contributed to the production of this volume. Several friends of Fr. Ken gave Igumen Iona expert medical treatment during his stay. Dr. Leo Uyeda gave him an eye examination and fitted him with new glasses. Dr. Richard Hansen took care of his dental health and filled his teeth. And Dr. Bruce Mutter ministered to his several physical ailments. We are grateful for their clinical expertise and their generous and compassionate hearts.

A special thanks to Dr. Janice Strength, a psychologist at Fuller Theological Seminary, who was able to get permission for Igumen Iona to attend classes there during his sojourn in Southern California. Her friendship and kindness were self-sacrificing and always generous.

Thanks to Mel Ahlborn, who reviewed our translation and found the book to be a "verbal icon showing forth the grace of God." Not only did Mel give us the benefit of her critique, but she continually encouraged Fr. Ken to find a publisher for this book.

And last, our thanks to Deacon Thomas Zell of Conciliar Press. He has shepherded this book into print so that you may experience its treasures. We are grateful for his good efforts.

ПУТЬ КО СПАСЕНІЮ.

(КРАТКІЙ ОЧЕРКЪ АСКЕТИКИ).

ТРЕТЬЯ ЧАСТЬ

НАЧЕРТАНІЯ ХРИСТІАНСКАГО НРАВОУЧЕНІЯ.

Сочиненіе Епископа Ѳеофана.

ИЗДАНІЕ ВОСЬМОЕ

Аѳонскаго Русскаго Пантелеимонова монастыри.

ОТДѢЛЪ I.

Послѣ общаго введенія, — О НАЧАЛѢ ХРИСТІАНСКОЙ ЖИЗНИ ЧРЕЗЪ СВ. КРЕЩЕНІЕ, съ указаніемъ—какъ сохранить сію благодать въ періодъ воспитанія.

МОСКВА.
Типо-Литографія И. Ефимова. Большая Якиманка, собственный домъ.
1899.

Cover of a Russian edition of The Path of Salvation, *printed in Moscow in 1899.*

Translator's Introduction

You have in your hands a book that is arguably the most profound work on repentance in all of Christendom. St. Theophan speaks not only from a deep knowledge of the Church Fathers, but also from a lifetime of experience in turning his heart to God, and guiding others on this glorious Way that leads to our salvation.

I first heard of this book by St. Theophan many years ago while reading a secondary work on Russian mystics. Having experienced the power of St. Theophan's writing and his ability to communicate the most profound mysteries in *The Art of Prayer* and *Unseen Warfare,* it was quite frustrating to know of this work but not to be able to read it. At that time, there was no English translation available. Then, in 1994 during one of my trips to Russia, I became friends with a Russian hieromonk, Igumen Iona, who was very familiar with this work. On a train going to Yaroslavl, we agreed to work together to translate this work into English.

After much difficulty, Igumen Iona came to California in October of 1995. We were able to work for six months before he had to return to Russia. During this time, we translated the first two books of Theophan's great magnum opus, *The Path of Salvation.* You have in your hands the second of the three parts. Originally published as three separate books, these volumes were combined in the late nineteenth century into one. Each of the three, however, stands alone.

Although this is Theophan's major work, *The Path of Salvation* has resisted translation because it is such an extremely difficult text in the original Russian. Theophan wrote in a special kind of high-philosophical language that was common to the late-nineteenth-century intelligentsia. With the repressions of the Soviet state, those who spoke and wrote this language were murdered, and the language is all but forgotten now. Igumen Iona sometimes had to translate Theophan's Russian into modern Russian to understand his meaning, and we would then translate the modern Russian rendering into English.

Another difficulty which complicates any translation is the profound difference between Russian and English thought processes. Languages are not just the use of different sounds for different objects. They are different ways of perceiving and understanding the world. They embody different ways of thinking. So our task was not just to convey a word-for-word equivalence, but to communicate the essence of Theophan's thought while remaining true to a literal rendering of his words. Given the importance of this subject matter to the reader's spiritual life, we rendered this book as literally as possible.

We translated from the 1899 facsimile edition published on Mount Athos. To achieve as much clarity as possible, Igumen Iona rendered the Russian text into English, with numerous variants for our mutual consideration. Then, after much discussion, we decided on the proper translation and I fashioned the text into clear, idiomatic English. We used footnotes liberally, so that the additions we made to clarify the text would not distract the reader from Theophan's thought.

Where biblical quotations appear in the text, they are Theophan's. Where they appear in footnotes, they are ours, added to show the biblical basis for the saint's teachings. We used the Revised Standard Version and the King James Version of scripture to stay close to the *feel* of Theophan's usage. Where there are italics in the text, they are those of Theophan or his editors.

When there were two shades of meaning in a Russian word and the context did not make clear which shade Theophan intended, we typically included both shades in the translation. We took great pains to be faithful to the meaning of the text and to convey, insofar as we could, what we believed to be Theophan's meaning. This text describes the very precise movements of the

Holy Spirit in redeeming sinners. It is thus a manual for spiritual transformation. We tried very hard to preserve this.

While striving our utmost to be faithful to Theophan's meaning, we have taken some liberties with breaking up long Russian sentences and long paragraphs. All of the subheadings which you see in the text are ours. Breaking up the text in this way makes it more accessible to the modern English reader without disturbing the meaning of the text.

Repentance is not a popular subject in the West. You will have to look hard to find any titles under this subject heading, despite the fact that repentance is the cornerstone of our Lord's gospel and the entrance into God's Kingdom for most of us. To learn the full meaning of repentance, we must go to those who have drunk deeply from this cup—those great holy ones of the Christian East. May you learn from St. Theophan, and may your efforts be richly rewarded in our Lord Jesus Christ.

Fr. Ken Kaisch
The Feast of St. Augustine, 2000

St. Theophan's Russia

THE CULTURAL CONTEXT

Nineteenth-century Russia was a culture in transition. At the beginning of the century, Russia was rudely invaded from the West by Napoleon and his armies in 1812. This awakened Russia from its self-absorption and presaged the need for modernization. But the Napoleonic invasion was only the outward sign of a series of more tempestuous invasions from the West.

Georges Florovsky describes this time as a time of "philosophical awakening" and "spiritual displacement."[1] In his revealing summary of this period of Russian history, he writes simply, "Thought awakened." Quoting Dostoevsky, Florovsky says that "it was a moment when 'we looked at ourselves consciously for the first time.' "[2]

The ideas of political and economic freedom which were being developed and implemented in the West, notably in the American and French revolutions, excited Russians of the upper classes, who were just awakening to philosophy. Their philosophical awakening was more than it seemed. It was as if "the individual" were being roused. Previously, Russia had been wholly under the sway of the communal. Now, however, a radical idea from the West—the notion of the individual and his importance—was challenging the time-honored values of Mother Russia. The ill-fated Decembrist insurrection of 1825 is a clear example of men who, though powerfully shaken by these new ideas of freedom, had not yet developed a capacity for the reasoned exploration of their ideas.

---

1   Florovsky, G., *The Ways of Russian Theology, Part II.* Vaduz, Europa: Buchervertriebsanstalt, 1987, p. 1.
2   Op. cit., p. 2.

The Decembrist insurrection brought to the fore a question which had long been simmering in the Russian consciousness: the question of the serfs. Russia was the last European country to free its peasant population from bondage to the land and its owners. As the tides of industrialization rose in Europe and as the military advantages of industrialization made themselves manifest, there was more and more tension within Russia over this issue. Without a labor force, there could be no industrialization. And without the freeing of the serfs—and the radical change of life that this would mean throughout all levels of Russian society—there could be no labor force to power the desired industrialization.

In 1855, the new tsar, Alexander II, decided upon the reformation of Russian society, and in 1861 he issued a decree freeing the serfs. The institution of peasant bondage, abolished in Western Europe hundreds of years previously, was no longer the bedrock upon which the economics of Holy Russia rested. For Alexander, this move was part of a desperate attempt to industrialize his nation. It had become increasingly clear that Russia could not defend its boundaries without an industrial base. And the key to industrialization was the freeing of farm laborers so that they could work in urban factories.

Thus, along with a revolution in the social and economic structure, there was a mass migration to the urban centers and to factory work. Russia took to this with great enthusiasm, and all of the wretched excesses that every industrialized country endures were present in Russia as well.

This destruction of the social fabric of the village and the creation of chaotic new urban centers resulted in an increasing crescendo of political unrest that finally climaxed in the Revolution of 1917. New democratic ideas about the equality of men were promulgated in the repressive autocratic atmosphere of tsarist Russia. Given the swiftness of the changes which Russia endured through the last half of the nineteenth century, the Revolution of 1917 should not surprise us.

THE SPIRITUAL CONTEXT

The Russian people were steadied through these massive social changes by the great protective bulwark of the Russian Orthodox Church. Rooted in the mysticism of the Christian faith and celebrating majestic liturgies which transported believers into the heavenly realm, the Russian Church provided a constant in the lives of her people. But even the Church was experiencing significant changes.

In the eighteenth and early nineteenth centuries, considerable restrictions had been placed on the Church, beginning with the decrees of Peter the Great. These decrees especially affected those men aspiring to the monastic vocation. Beginning with Peter the Great, the Russian state needed soldiers for its armies, not "useless monastics." As a result, decrees were promulgated so that the state controlled who could become a monastic, and few were allowed this vocation. In this repressive environment arose St. Paisius Velichkovsky (1722–1794).

ST. PAISIUS VELICHKOVSKY

Desiring not only the tonsure of a monk, but also the guidance of an experienced spiritual elder, Paisius had to leave Russia to achieve his aspirations, first going to Moldavia (1742) and then to Mount Athos (1746) in Greece. Monasticism was at such a low ebb that he had great difficulty in finding the spiritual guidance he desired. On his way to a monastery in Moldavia, Paisius heard of Elder Basil from one of Basil's disciples, Fr. Michael. Basil was described as "a man most experienced in the understanding of divine Scripture and the teaching of the God-bearing fathers and in spiritual discernment."[3] Attracted by this description, Paisius met Elder Basil and stayed in the sketes that were under the spiritual direction of this elder from 1742 to 1746. Several years later, in 1750, Elder Basil visited Paisius on Mount Athos, where the elder

---

3   Quoted in *Elder Basil of Poina Marului*. Liberty, TN: St. John of Kronstadt Press, 1996, p. 12.

tonsured him and gave him the name of his deceased coworker, Paisius.

At the instruction of Elder Basil, Paisius broke his solitude and began accepting disciples. In time, his example was so stirring that thousands flocked to his monastery, and he served many as their spiritual elder. So Paisius did not just rest with the matter of his own salvation. He took the grace that he had received and directed that powerful stream back into Russia, into the hearts of his countrymen.

Paisius was remarkable in two respects. First, he became acquainted with the Jesus Prayer in Greece, and became the conduit for its transmission into Holy Russia. From this simple beginning, the use of the Jesus Prayer swept through the Russian monastic community and from there, it seeped into the mass of the laity with enormous effect. Second, Paisius began the great labor of translating the early Church Fathers from Greek into Russian. He was the first Russian translator of the *Philokalia* and, in addition, translated numerous patristic texts. This work became the foundation of a deeply spiritual reform which raced through the Russian monasteries of the nineteenth century.

ST. SERAPHIM OF SAROV

Paisius' work bore immediate fruit in the person of St. Seraphim of Sarov (1759–1833). The son of a stonemason and brickmaker, Seraphim had a number of remarkable spiritual occurrences in his childhood. At seventeen he left his family for the monastery, and spent the first part of his monastic career in ascetic labors. These included the practice of the Jesus Prayer, solitude, and fasting of the most severe sort. Through his use of the Jesus Prayer and the other spiritual disciplines of the early Fathers, Seraphim was an indirect inheritor of St. Paisius' works.

After a long period of ascetic labors, Seraphim began to receive and counsel visitors. He manifested such grace and perception that people from all over Russia sought his counsel, even including Tsar Alexander I. Seraphim became known as a wonder-worker for the miraculous healings which took place in his presence, for his clairvoyance, and for his sage advice, which helped many in their spiritual journeys. St. Seraphim became known far and wide, and served as a spiritual beacon for the faithful. Through his ascetic labors, the faithful could see what a difference deep faith in Christ and a holy life could make.

THE OPTINA ELDERS

During the nineteenth century, a monastery arose that became even more famous than Sarov. This was the monastery of Optina, with its succession of great spiritual elders: Moses, Isaac, Leonid, Anthony, Macarius, Hilarion, Ambrose, Joseph, Barsanuphius, and Anatole. These elders stood in the line of direct transmission from St. Paisius. Their "school" began with the work of Moses Putilov, who knew St. Seraphim at Sarov and who was the spiritual son of Fr. Athanasius, a direct disciple of St. Paisius.

The elders of Optina were notable in several respects. First, they received and transmitted the living tradition of the Jesus Prayer and the practical lore that had been gathered by generations of previous practitioners. They served as a kind of deep spiritual well from which travelers from all over Russia drew the living water of contemplative prayer.

Second, they instituted a practice known as the *confession of thoughts*. This practice is the daily confession to one's elder of those thoughts that were sinful. More rigorous than the confession of sinful deeds, the confession of thoughts cuts off sinful impulses before they become manifest in outward behavior. This practice inhibited those behaviors destructive to the spiritual life and had a salutary effect on the lives of the Optina elders and others who practiced it.

Third, these elders continued in the Paisian tradition of translating and publishing the works of the early Fathers of the Church. Thus, through Optina, the deepest spiritual heritage of Orthodoxy was made available throughout the Church in Russia. This was of equal importance to their work of spiritual eldering. By serving thousands in the direction of souls, they greatly influenced a generation. But through their work of translation, they have influenced many generations, and helped to keep the faith alive during the years of the communist persecution of the faithful.

Thus, despite the series of tumultuous changes in the social, economic, and political fabric of nineteenth-century Russia, the Church remained a shining beacon for its people. This is not to say that the Church did not have its difficulties. It was too closely identified with the tsarist state, and suffered from the usual political intrigues of any state-connected church. Nevertheless, it also offered stability for its people in an increasingly stormy sea of changes, and a vision of life that was increasingly at odds with the new life that was roaring in from the West.

THE SPIRITUAL LINEAGE OF ST. THEOPHAN

This was the political, social, and spiritual climate from which Theophan arose. Born directly after the Napoleonic invasion, raised in this changing political and social atmosphere, he was a true Russian son of these changes. Due to his desire for a spiritual life and to his brilliant intellect, he was schooled in the most advanced theological academies of his time. Then, unlike most Russian clerics of his time, he went to the Holy Land on the first Russian mission there. There his early learning was both expanded and deepened.

Theophan's learning was expanded by contact with numerous cultures very different from his own. He experienced firsthand the culture of the Ottoman Turks, the indigenous Arabic culture, and on his journey home, the cultures of Italy and Germany. Thus, he saw the multitude of different ways in which Christianity had been adapted to different peoples and cultures. He saw the strengths and the errors of these adaptations, and was better able to understand, as a result, the core of the Christian faith and journey.

Theophan was also deepened in ways that we can never fully know. He was privileged to visit some of the most ancient monasteries of Christendom in Syria, the Sinai, and Egypt. There he made copies of the works of the great spiritual giants of Christianity, which he carried back to Russia. We can see, from his translating activities later in life, his devotion to the transmission of this wisdom. He went into reclusion, not just for his own prayer life, but to better serve the Church by engaging in and directing a vast work of translation. His efforts, in conjunction with those of the Optina elders, brought to Russia the timeless wisdom of the ancients.

Theophan's major work, *The Way to Salvation,* is both an exceedingly *traditional* book and one that is quite *contemporary.* It is traditional in that it rests solidly on the Holy Scriptures and the writings of the Church Fathers. It is contemporary in that the psychological aspects of the ascetic way are clearly delineated. The psychological states and changes that occur throughout the spiritual journey are described in enough detail that you can recognize your own experience. As a result, this book can serve as a kind of spiritual guide for those who travel on the Way. This is the greatest value of this book.

This is also the purpose for which Theophan intended this volume. The original audience for the material contained in *The Path of Salvation* consisted of seminarians at the foremost theological school in Russia. These students were the cream of the cream. Theophan's purpose was to guide those who heard the call of God in their walk on the way to salvation. The book is therefore a workbook—a spiritual traveler's guidebook. There are not many such books in any language.

St. Theophan

The Life of St. Theophan the Recluse
(1815–1894)

Most people of the present era devote themselves to a ceaseless round of external activities. The world has undergone such a revolution since World War II that everyone now runs after money and power. The struggle to obtain these precious commodities absorbs all our time and our energy. Everything has been reduced to money; nothing else seems to have value. Art is valued, not for its beauty, but for the high prices it commands. Integrity and character are not valued at all.

As the horror and emptiness of the primary values of our era reveal themselves ever more clearly, a contrasting pool of light is more and more sharply delineated. In this light stand those great souls who have ordered their lives around a different set of values. These are people who have disengaged from the outer world in order to plunge more fully into the inner world. These are intrepid explorers of the soul, those whom we call saints. They do not trumpet their activities to the world. Rather, they manifest an extraordinary love which heals the wounds of those lost in pursuit of the world's values. By their lives and their teaching, they direct those who are overcome by the emptiness of the outer life into the living depths of Love. St. Theophan the Recluse belongs to this group of deeply spiritual persons.

BEGINNINGS

Bishop Theophan, known in the secular world as George Govorov, was born on January 10, 1815, in the village of Chernavskoje in the province of Orjol. His father, Basil, was a priest of the parish church in that village. At the age of eight, George entered the ecclesiastical school in Livny, and at fourteen, he was promoted to Orjol Theological Seminary. Having finished seminary in 1837 with excellent marks, George received an appointment to study at the Kiev Theological Academy.

Kiev was the birthplace of Christianity in Russia and also the birthplace of Russian monasticism. A community of monks had been established in caves near Kiev from the first days of Christianity in Russia. This monastery has been in existence since those early days, broken only during the Soviet period. George was greatly influenced by the monks of the Kiev Caves Lavra.[1] In this place, the ancient spiritual traditions were kept alive. Here there were true witnesses who participated fully in the ancient traditions of heroic spiritual exploits. As a young student, George often went to the Kiev Caves Lavra. He experienced extraordinary manifestations of God's grace in that place. These spiritual experiences were so deep and so powerful that even at the end of his life, he remembered them with delight. "Kiev Lavra is an unearthly (heavenly) abode."[2] During this time, his spiritual father was a monk of the lavra, Schemamonk Partheny of Kiev. Partheny was widely recognized as one of the true spiritual elders of his time. His influence on the young, impressionable student must have been powerful.

In the last year of his studies at the Academy, at the age of twenty-five, George made up his mind to devote himself to God by serving the Church as a monk. He was tonsured a monk on February 15, 1841, with the name of Theophan, in honor of St. Theophan the Confessor of Sigriane (March 12/25). In April 1841 the monk Theophan was ordained a hierodeacon in the main Dormition Cathedral of Kiev Caves Lavra, and on July 1 of the same year he was ordained a hieromonk.[3] Continuing his studies

---

1   *Lavra* is the Russian word for the most important central monasteries. There are only three lavras in Russia: that in Kiev, St. Sergius Lavra outside of Moscow, and Alexander Nevsky Lavra in St. Petersburg.

2   *Codfame nucek claretheteuil Theophana.* Bruyckthetuu, M. 1898, c 33.

3   A monastic priest.

at the Academy, he graduated in 1841 with a Master's degree in Theology.

Immediately upon his graduation, on August 27, 1841, Hieromonk Theophan was appointed headmaster of an ecclesiastical school, and shortly thereafter, as the inspector of Novgorod Theological Seminary, a position of considerable responsibility. By the age of twenty-nine, he was promoted to the Saint Petersburg Theological Academy and was assigned to the faculty of the Department of Moral and Pastoral Theology. This was the foremost theological institution in the Russian Empire at that time. From this quick rise, it is clear that Theophan's abilities were highly regarded by the Church authorities.

About his understanding of how to prepare for the responsibilities of an educator, Theophan writes, "An educator should experience all the stages of Christian perfection in order to know in his subsequent activity how to behave and be able to notice the inclinations of his pupils, and then to influence them with patience, successfully, strongly, and fruitfully. Such educators should be a class of the purest, chosen by God, and saintly persons."[4] Thus we see that, in his pedagogical activity, the young theologian did not use the speculative methods or rely solely on books. Rather, he based his teaching on the Christian ascetic and psychological experience, which he recapitulated in his own person.

Hieromonk Theophan was not greatly pleased by the administrative duties of his office. He had a profound distaste for such work and, in his heart of hearts, was not satisfied with this service. "The duties of my office fill me with nausea and distract me from church. The true paradise is there. When I come to the church, I have the feeling that this is the place to remain forever." Such were the longings in this young man's heart for God and God alone.

---

4   The unreferenced quotations of Theophan in this biography are taken from an article about the saint's life that was published in the beginning of the twentieth century. At that time, referenced quotations were not obligatory. We suppose that this and the following unreferenced quotations are taken from St. Theophan's letters.

THEOPHAN'S JOURNEY TO THE HOLY LAND

An opportunity for satisfying his spiritual needs soon arose for Hieromonk Theophan. On August 21, 1847, in accordance with his desire, he was appointed a member of the Russian Ecclesiastical Mission to Jerusalem. He left Russia and sojourned in the Holy Land for the next six years.

The purpose of this mission was to investigate the state of Orthodoxy in the Middle East, and to establish a permanent Russian ecclesiastical presence there. Based in Jerusalem, members of this mission traveled throughout the area, especially to Syria, Egypt, Sinai, and Mount Athos. This six-year sojourn in the East had great spiritual importance for Hieromonk Theophan. During this time, he visited the ancient monasteries of the Holy Land, where he studied the manuscripts of the early Church Fathers. Much of his work was done in the library of St. Sabas Monastery in Palestine and St. Catherine's Monastery on Mt. Sinai. He acquainted himself with the order and regulations of the Palestinian monasteries and with the lives of the great ascetics who had dwelt there. In addition, the young ascetic Theophan established close spiritual relationships with the elders of Athos by correspondence. They had a beneficial influence on the direction of his spiritual life and later helped him publish his works.

During these six years, Hieromonk Theophan learned Greek, Hebrew, Arabic, and French.[5] All of this occurred in conjunction with his other, considerable duties. His scholarly efforts here were to bear fruit later, during the period of his seclusion. Georges Florovsky, with his uncanny eye for discerning what is truly important, writes about Theophan's participation in the following way: "The journey to the East proved to be a major event in Theophan's life, extending his ecclesiastical horizons and endowing his world view with an ecumenical courage, a great spiritual

---

5   Bolshakoff, S. *Russian Mystics.* Kalamazoo, MI: Cistercian Publications, 1980, p. 198.

freedom and suppleness, a freedom from cultural context."[6] This mission came to an end with the eruption of the Crimean War in 1853, and in 1854 all the members of the mission were recalled from Jerusalem to Russia. On the way home, the delegation spent considerable time in Italy and Germany, so Theophan became acquainted firsthand with the Church in the West.

RECOGNITION AND PROMOTION

For his service on the mission, Hieromonk Theophan was raised to the rank of archimandrite on April 4, 1855. He was quickly appointed as a lecturer in canon law at St. Petersburg Theological Academy and, six months later, as the rector of Olonets Theological Seminary. On June 13, 1857, by the decree of the Most Holy Synod of the Russian Orthodox Church, Archimandrite Theophan was appointed as rector of the St. Petersburg Theological Academy. Thus at forty-two years of age, Theophan became the most important theological educator in the Russian Empire.

A scant two years later, in 1859, the Church authorities decided to raise Archimandrite Theophan to the rank of Bishop for the Diocese of Tambov and Shatsk. Bishop Theophan served only four years in the Tambov diocese, but in the course of such a short period he proved to be a zealous minister in all spheres of church life. During one of his pastoral journeys in the diocese, Bishop Theophan came to the hermitage[7] at Visha and greatly liked it for its order and regulations, for its location, which was very suitable for the solitary life, and for its beautiful surroundings. "There is nothing better in the whole world than Visha," he wrote later. Sometime later, when appointing Igumen[8] Arkady to be Father

---

6   Florovsky, G. *Ways of Russian Theology, Part II.* Vaduz, Europa: Buchervertriebsanstalt, 1987, p. 170.
7   In Russian usage, the word *hermitage* refers to those monasteries that are in the most remote locations. It is important not to confuse this with the common English usage—the cell of a single hermit.
8   An ecclesiastical rank in the Orthodox Church, between hieromonk and archimandrite. An igumen typically will be given charge of a small monastery.

Superior of Visha, Theophan at parting told him prophetically: "Go there, Father Igumen, and then, God willing, I will come to you."

When he was forty-six, Theophan was among those official church representatives who were present at the opening of the holy relics of St. Tikhon of Zadonsk and his subsequent canonization. The body of St. Tikhon was exhumed, and his coffin opened. Those present witnessed that Tikhon's relics were preserved by the Holy Spirit without corruption. This experience profoundly moved Theophan, and shaped the rest of his life. Barely five years later, he, like Bishop Tikhon before him, retired from public life and went into seclusion to serve God with even more intensity.

On July 22, 1863, Bishop Theophan was transferred to the ancient and much larger diocese of Vladimir and Suzdal. In the report of the Holy Synod it was written that Theophan "by his present ministry has acquired the necessary experience to rule so numerous a flock." Bishop Theophan was an excellent preacher, and did much to improve the standards among the clergy of his diocese. Unlike many prelates, he lived very simply. He dressed plainly and ate only one meal a day. Concerned for education, he founded a school for girls and many parish schools. He tried in everything to teach his people the way leading to salvation.

But the vast practical activities of ruling a diocese were not dear to Theophan's heart. From his youth he had longed for solitude. He remembered later, "From my youngest days I sought after and prayed that no one would prevent me from being with God constantly." And now, after twenty-five years of serving the Church through different posts and activities, Bishop Theophan found it opportune to realize his constant yearning. Having asked advice of Metropolitan Isidor of St. Petersburg, his old spiritual guide from his days at the Orjol Theological Academy, he petitioned the Holy Synod for retirement with the right to live in Visha Hermitage in the Tambov diocese. The Holy Synod granted his petition, and on July 17, 1866, he was released from his duties as diocesan bishop and appointed Father Superior of Visha Hermitage.

Left: Theophan, during the time he was Bishop of Vladimir.
Below: Vladimir, in the nineteenth century.

Top: Visha, in the nineteenth century.
Below: St. Theophan's house in Visha.

RETIREMENT AT VISHA

When Bishop Theophan arrived in Visha at the age of fifty-one, he found a large and vigorous monastery with about one hundred monks. The outward conditions at Visha were quite suitable for the spiritual needs of the ascetic Theophan. Visha Hermitage was situated far from large and noisy towns in a beautiful forest at the confluence of two rivers, the Tsna and the Visha. The monastery followed the cenobitic system,[9] and its regulations and customs were distinguished by their austerity and strictness. "It is so quiet at our monastery," wrote Bishop Theophan, "that it is worthy of astonishment." To the end of his life the bishop felt quite happy in Visha. "One may exchange Visha only for the Kingdom of Heaven."

The position of superior of the monastery, however, disturbed Theophan's peace. Thus, shortly after his arrival at Visha, he petitioned the Holy Synod again, this time for release from this position. The Synod granted this petition. The long-awaited solitude Bishop Theophan had desired so persistently came at last.

Shortly thereafter Theophan drew up a program for his work, including the translation of important works from the Greek Fathers and his own writing. He did not seclude himself from society during his first six years in the monastery. He willingly received visitors who came for his spiritual advice and instruction, went for walks, and sometimes, although very seldom, departed from the monastery for short periods.

Prayer was his main occupation during these first years at the monastery. He kept firmly in mind the precept of his spiritual father—Schemamonk Partheny of Kiev—that "one thing is the most important and necessary, namely to pray, and to pray to God constantly with all one's mind and heart."

With the monks of the monastery he regularly attended all

---

9   The cenobitic monastic system is based on monks or nuns living in community in a monastery. It is in contrast with the other major monastic path, the eremitic system of living as a recluse or a hermit.

the services, and on Sundays and feast days he celebrated the Divine Liturgy together with the brethren. He participated fully in the church services, and often stood without moving and with his eyes closed, so as not to be distracted from the prayer of his heart. Before his seclusion, Theophan occasionally became totally immersed in prayer. During services, after he had received communion, the *antidoron* would be brought to him. Theophan would be standing so totally immersed in prayer that it would be several minutes before he became aware that someone was waiting for him.[10]

At the beginning of his sojourn in Visha, it was difficult to leave the world completely, and there were temptations to return. It is reported that Theophan was offered the position of metropolitan, one of the ruling bishops of the Russian Orthodox Church. But these were transient temptations for Theophan, and he put them aside to concentrate on his work of spiritual direction, writing, and translation.

However rigorously Theophan limited his intercourse with the world, nevertheless it distracted his attention from the main purposes for which he had come to Visha. As a result, he began to think about complete seclusion. This, however, was not realized all at once, but only gradually. First Theophan spent the whole of one Great Lent in absolute seclusion, and this experiment was successful. Then he secluded himself for an entire year. This provided him with the tranquility necessary to continue and deepen his work, and so Bishop Theophan came to the stillness he had desired so persistently throughout his life.

TOTAL SECLUSION

In 1872, after the days of Easter, Bishop Theophan distributed his belongings to the poor and began the life of a recluse. He broke

---

10   The *antidoron* is the blessed bread from the communion service, which is customarily taken to the clergy and participants. As the superior of the monastery, Theophan would have been the first to receive the antidoron, so his absorption in prayer would have been noticeable to the whole community.

at 57

off all personal contact with people and ceased attending the divine services with the brethren. From 1872 to the end of his life, he received only the Father Superior of the monastery, Archimandrite Arkady; his spiritual father, Igumen Tikhon; and his cell-assistant, Father Evlampy. With all the others who longed to receive his spiritual guidance, he continued his conversations by means of correspondence only.

HIS LIFE OF PRAYER

In Theophan's understanding, seclusion was for the purpose of unceasing prayer. "What is seclusion for?" wrote Theophan. "It is when the mind, having enclosed itself in the heart, stands before God with veneration and does not want to go out of the heart or concern itself with anything else."

Theophan's prayer labor revolved around the celebration of the Divine Liturgy. Bishop Theophan had established a chapel in his rooms and consecrated it in honor of the Epiphany.[11] In this cell-church he celebrated the Divine Liturgy on Sundays and on the feast days. During the last eleven years of his life, he celebrated the Liturgy every day. He always performed the service alone, usually in silence, but at times chanting aloud. The monks of the monastery were of the opinion that Bishop Theophan performed the Liturgy according to the rule of the hermits of Palestine and Mount Athos, which was familiar to him from his experience as a member of the Mission in Jerusalem. During the day, at the proper times, he chanted the rest of the monastic services (vespers, midnight service, matins, and hours). When he could not conduct the services, he replaced them with the Jesus Prayer.

Bishop Theophan was constantly in meditation and prompted others to do the same. "Don't deviate from God in your mind," he wrote in one of his letters, "whether you are praying or doing something else." Theophan kept himself in a state of constant, uninterrupted meditation, mainly by reading the Holy Scriptures

---

11 In Greek, the words Epiphany and Theophany refer to the same event, the showing forth of the Christ to the world in the event of His Baptism.

and books of the Church Fathers. In his cell he had one of the largest private libraries in Russia. There were books from all branches of human knowledge in Hebrew, Greek, Latin, German, French, English, and other languages.

HIS WRITING AND CORRESPONDENCE

Bishop Theophan's literary activities were truly heroic. Second only to his prayer life, Theophan devoted himself to an extended ministry to the Church by means of his writing and correspondence. According to his own acknowledgment, not infrequently he spent "day and night" in this work. In addition, Theophan struggled with cataracts in both eyes in his later years. Twice he left Visha for treatment of these cataracts, but without result. At the age of 73, he became blind in one eye, but continued his work.[12]

Bishop Theophan saw his seclusion as an opportunity to minister to the wider Church through his writings. The silence and ordered life that he created for himself in seclusion served to assist him as he penetrated more and more deeply into the mysteries of prayer and the spiritual life. This sacrifice of himself enabled him to draw closer to God than was possible amidst the distractions of service in the world. We are blessed, even today, to receive the continuing fruits of his ascetic and literary labors.

Theophan's literary efforts can be grouped into three main areas. First, he continued to direct spiritual seekers by means of a voluminous correspondence. "For very many people he became a correspondent-confessor."[13] He received twenty to forty letters every day, and answered them all faithfully. This, by itself, would be an extraordinary feat. His correspondence has been gathered together and partially published. The most important collections of his letters have been published under the titles, *The Spiritual Life and How to Be Attuned to It*[14] and *Letters on the Christian Life,*

---

12   Bolshakoff, p. 202. This information was not readily available from Russian sources, but found only in Bolshakoff.

13   Florovsky, p. 169.

14   St. Theophan the Recluse. *The Spiritual Life and How to Be Attuned to It.* Forestville, CA: St. Herman of Alaska Brotherhood Press, 1995.

adapted from his correspondence with Princess P. S. Lukomskaia.[15]

Second, and in addition to his prodigious correspondence, Theophan translated into Russian books that he thought might be edifying for his countrymen. These included five volumes of *The Philokalia, Ancient Monastic Statutes, Unseen Warfare,* and *The Sermons of St. Symeon the New Theologian. The Philokalia* alone took twenty years to translate completely.

Finally, Theophan wrote books of his own. The volume on repentance which you are now holding is taken from his major work, *The Path of Salvation.* His other works, which have not been translated, include: *On Prayer and Vigilance; On Penance, Communion and Reformation of Life;* and commentaries on all of the Epistles of St. Paul (with the exception of the Letter to the Hebrews), and on several of the psalms. In English, there is an excellent book, *The Art of Prayer,*[16] which is compiled mostly from the works of Theophan.

The principal theme of Theophan's writings was salvation in Christ. The works of the Eastern Church Fathers and ascetics were the foundation for his understanding in these matters. His writings were both comprehensive in their completeness and faithful in their reflection of the spirit and nature of the ascetic views of the Fathers. Bishop Theophan was widely acknowledged as "a genuine and typical continuer of patristic tradition in asceticism and theology."[17]

The works of the Recluse of Visha are not the fruit of a theoretical or speculative theologian,[18] but the experience of an active ascetic who built his spiritual life on the rock of the Holy Scriptures and Holy Traditions of the Church. "We know," wrote

---

15 Florovsky, p. 171.

16 This book is not Theophan's title, and contains material from several other authors. Igumen Chariton. *The Art of Prayer: An Orthodox Anthology.* Boston, MA: Faber and Faber, 1966.

17 Florovsky, p. 169.

18 To understand the use of the word *theologian* in the Orthodox tradition, we need to remember the inseparable link between prayer and theology. Theology is the direct intuitive knowledge of God, acquired by means of an active spiritual life.

Professor A. Brouzov, "not a single theologian who would be penetrated with biblical and patristic spirit to such an extent, as that which is so obvious in every line of Bishop Theophan. One can say with certainty that all his moral teaching is biblical and patristic. And in this is his greatest merit."

OTHER ACTIVITIES

Theophan alternated his prayer and writing with different kinds of handiwork, according to the custom of the Desert Fathers. It refreshed him, and above all, it banished any thoughts of idleness. The bishop occupied himself with painting, woodcarving, lathe work, and bookbinding. For these occupations there were several boxes with the necessary tools in his study. Besides that there were a telescope, two microscopes, a camera, an anatomical atlas, and six atlases of geography and history in his cell.

Theophan especially liked icon-painting. After his death, there were found in his cell many icons and pictures of sacred history that he had painted. While in seclusion, Theophan decided to learn how to play musical instruments. For this purpose, he ordered a harmonium and then a violin, together with self-instruction manuals and sheet music for different spiritual compositions.

Although Theophan secluded himself from society, he did not lose interest in national and international events; he willingly responded to the most significant events in the public life of his native land. He was sharply critical of the moral and spiritual decline which he saw throughout Russia. He constantly exhorted the hierarchs and clergy to reform before true Orthodoxy was lost. In this way, he seemed to see prophetically into the future and to have some foreknowledge of the events coming to Russia in 1917 and following.

Theophan was widely recognized in his own day. The Church throughout Russia felt and appreciated his efforts through his literary output, despite his reclusion and isolation in the forests of Visha. He continued to receive honors and acclaim. Over the course of his life in reclusion, he was elected as an honorary member of all of the theological academies of the Russian Orthodox Church. In 1890, four years before his death, the St. Petersburg Academy awarded him an honorary doctorate of divinity.

HIS BIRTHDAY INTO ETERNITY

Bishop Theophan was remarkably healthy until his end. Five days before his death, there were changes in his schedule. Professor P. A. Smirnov described Theophan's last days.

> On the eve of his death, January 5, his Lordship, feeling weak, asked for help to walk. The keleinik[19] assisted Bishop Theophan for a few turns around the room. But his Lordship, quickly becoming tired, sent the keleinik away and went to bed. On the day of Theophan's death, the keleinik, hearing no accustomed knock, looked into the study of the bishop at 1 P.M. The bishop was sitting and writing something . . . . After half an hour, there was a slight knock. During the meal, the bishop consumed half of an egg and drank half of the glass of milk. Hearing no knock for tea, the keleinik looked in at 4:30 P.M. The bishop was lying in bed . . . dead. His left hand rested on his breast while the right was formed as for the episcopal blessing. When the bishop was pontifically vested,[20] a smile clearly appeared on his face.[21]

Bishop Theophan died in peace on the feast day of the Theophany, January 6/19, 1894. His body was placed in his cell-chapel for three days. Then for another three days it was placed in the cathedral. During this time, there was no smell of corruption. A great crowd of people from all over Russia came for his funeral.

---

19   *Keleinik* means cell-attendant, the person who would assist the recluse. Bishop Theophan's keleinik was Fr. Evlampy, who served him for twenty-five years.
20   That is, robed in his ceremonial vestments as a bishop, as is the custom in the Orthodox Church before interment.
21   Bolshakoff, p. 202.

We know very little of Theophan's life in reclusion. It is often the case that the world learns of the ascetic feats of a holy one like Theophan by means of the reports of the cell-attendant after the death of the ascetic. We do not have this in Theophan's case. His cell-attendant of twenty-five years, Father Evlampy, fasted for ten days after the bishop's death and died within two weeks of Theophan's passing. It was as if he could not bear to remain on earth without the sweetness of the blessed one whom he had served.

POSTLUDE

In accordance with his will, all of Theophan's manuscripts were sent to the library at the Monastery of St. Panteleimon on Mount Athos. Given the events which befell Russia subsequently, this foresight was blessed. Unfortunately, at the present time these manuscripts are deteriorating due to the poor conditions in the monastery library.

After the Russian Revolution of 1917, the monastery at Visha was closed in 1924 and the monks were exiled to an unknown fate. The monastery buildings were later turned into a mental hospital by the communists. Theophan's relics were moved to a nearby village church, where they remain to this day.

In 1988, the Russian Orthodox Church convened a council for the whole Church in Russia to celebrate the millennium of Christianity in their country. At this celebration, which took place June 6–9, 1988, the Russian Church formally recognized the sanctity of Bishop Theophan, and he was canonized. Known now as St. Theophan the Recluse, he is with us still to guide us along that great way which leads to our salvation.

Pray for us, Holy Father Theophan,
who still journey on the Way

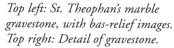

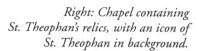

Top left: St. Theophan's marble gravestone, with bas-relief images.
Top right: Detail of gravestone.

Right: Chapel containing St. Theophan's relics, with an icon of St. Theophan in background.

Left: A modern icon of St. Theophan.

St. Theophan's Introduction

The main task on the way to salvation is to live in the spirit of Christ. Anyone who broaches this subject will at once encounter many questions, and many perplexities will be uncovered. That is why it is necessary to explain nearly every step of this way!

Man's final goal is communion with God. The way to this goal lies through faith in Christ, together with constantly keeping His commandments with the assistance of God's grace. One needs only to say in addition, "This is the way! Follow it."

It is easy to say this, but how is one to do it? For the most part, people have no desire to move in this direction. Their souls, pulled by one passion or another, stubbornly refuse every gentle invitation and every call. The soul averts its gaze from God and does not want to look at Him. The law of Christ does not conform to the soul's liking. The soul does not have a disposition even to hear this law. As the saying goes, "The soul has a distaste for Christ's law."

The questions to be addressed in this book are:

1   How does one reach the point where the desire is born to move towards God by way of Christ?

2   What does one do so that the Law imprints itself, not just as ink on paper, but as the Spirit of the living God imprints itself on the living flesh of the heart?[1]

3   How can a man act according to this Law willingly and unconstrainedly, as if it came from himself, so that this law does not lie on him like a burden, but proceeds from his deepest nature?

If someone has turned towards God, and has come to love His Law, is this enough to insure the success of the journey? Is this turning the same as walking the path of Christ's law? Will the journey be successful merely because we desire it? No.

---

1   Cf. 2 Corinthians 3:3

In addition to the desire, it is necessary to have the strength and the ability to act—that is, active wisdom.[2] Whoever enters this true way of pleasing God, whoever begins with the help of grace to strive towards God in the way of Christ's law, will inevitably be threatened by the danger of losing his way at the crossroads,[3] of going astray and perishing while under the illusion that he is working out his salvation. These crossroads are unavoidable because of our sinful inclinations and the disorder of our faculties,[4] even in those who are converted.[5] These sinful inclinations and disordered faculties are capable of presenting things to a man in a false light, and deceiving and destroying the man.

Moreover, in addition to these things,[6] there is flattery from Satan,[7] who is reluctant to leave his victims. When someone under his authority goes to the light of Christ, Satan pursues him and sets every manner of trap in order to catch him again. Not infrequently he succeeds. Consequently the spiritual traveler who already has the desire to follow the way to the Lord must be informed of all the possible deviations, so that he may be warned beforehand, may see the dangers that are to be encountered, and may learn how to avoid them.

These unavoidable things, which are encountered on the way to salvation and are common for everyone, require special guiding principles that are indispensable for the Christian life. These

2 Active wisdom is the practical knowledge of how to act. The Russian term, *mudrost' deiatel'naya,* is derived from the Greek *praxis,* and refers to the ability of a person to act in accordance with the knowledge and understanding which is given to him by God, and *to put into practice* this understanding. It is a wisdom of practice and action, of doing what we know to be right. God gives us the grace of wisdom, but it is our part to find that wisdom within ourselves, and put that wisdom into practice.

3 Theophan here speaks figuratively. These crossroads are the places where we must choose between the right way and all other ways. Often we are not conscious of these crossroads; we come to them and choose without knowing, or we choose the wrong way thinking that it is the right way.

4 The term *faculties* of a person refers to the powers of reason, imagination, will, consciousness, attention, memory, and understanding.

5 Cf. Romans 7:25

6 That is, our sinful inclinations and disordered faculties.

7 Cf. 2 Timothy 2:26 and 1 Peter 5:8

principles define how to acquire the saving desire for communion with God, the fervent desire[8] to remain in communion with Him, and how to come to God safely through all the crossroads that must be negotiated on the way and at every stage on the way. In other words, how to begin to live the Christian life and how, having begun, to perfect oneself in it.

These guiding principles must take the man who is separated from God, turn him towards God, and then bring him into God's Presence. They must show to the man the practical development of the Christian life in all its manifestations and levels, from its very beginning to the end. That is how the Christian life is sown, germinates, develops, and becomes mature. In other words, we must give an account of the unfolding of the active life[9] for every Christian, to show how he must act in every possible case so that he may stand firm in his calling.

The sowing, germination, and development of the Christian life differs in essence from the sowing, germination, and development of the natural life. This difference is the result of the special character of the Christian life and its relationship to our human nature. A man is not born a Christian, but becomes such after birth. The seed of Christ falls on the soil of a heart that is already beating. Since the natural man is fallen, he is opposed to the demands of Christianity. In a plant, however, the beginning of life is the stirring of a sprout in the seed, an awakening of dormant powers. The beginning of a true Christian life in a man is a kind

---

8   The Russian term *r'evnost'* would have been translated as *zeal* in St. Theophan's time. However, *zeal* has a somewhat negative connotation in current English usage, a connotation that would be completely foreign to Theophan and his contemporaries. Consequently, we prefer to translate this technical spiritual term as *fervent desire.* Due to the flow of the translation, it has not always proven possible to do so, so the reader will find an alternation between *zeal, fervent desire,* and *active desire.*

9   The word which we have translated here as *active life*—in Russian, *deiatel'naya zhizn'*—is used in a technical sense, and refers to the practical, active life of a Christian, as opposed to an intellectual Christianity. Sometimes you hear a person say that he/she is a Christian, but not a practicing Christian. Theophan would understand that this person is not truly a Christian, but merely under the illusion that he is Christian.

of re-creation and rebirth, an endowment of new powers and of new life.[10]

Furthermore, although Christianity is accepted as law—that is, the resolution is made to live a Christian life—this seed of life (this resolution) is not surrounded in a man by conditions favorable to it.[11] At this time the whole man, in his body and soul, remains ill-adapted to the new life, refractory and not submissive to the yoke of Christ.[12] From the moment of decision, a man begins hard labor, the labor to educate his whole self and all his faculties according to the Christian standard.

That is why, whereas with the growth of plants, for example, there is a gradual development of the powers[13] of the plant in an easy, unconstrained way, it is not so with a Christian. Rather, he has a hard struggle with himself, intense and sorrowful, and he must dispose his faculties towards things for which they have no natural inclination. Like a warrior, he must win every inch of land, even his own, from his enemies by means of warfare.[14] He must use the two-edged sword of self-constraint and self-coercion. Finally, after long and hard labors and exertions, Christian principles emerge victorious, reigning without opposition. Having dislodged the demands and inclinations which are hostile to humanity from the whole of human nature, these principles penetrate our nature and place it in a state of purity and freedom from passions. These principles bestow upon a man the bliss of those who are pure in heart, so that the man can see God in himself in the most sincere communion with Him.

Such is the condition in us of the Christian life. It has three stages, which, according to their characteristics, we may describe as follows:

---

10   Cf. John 3:3; Romans 6:1–11
11   Cf. Ephesians 6:10–20
12   Cf. Matthew 11:29, 30
13   English speakers do not typically think of plants as having powers. Theophan here speaks of the powers of vegetative life: the power of a seed, for example, to break through a concrete slab, or to split a rock.
14   Cf. Ephesians 6:10–20

1   turning to God, which is conversion;
2   purification or self-amendment; and
3   sanctification.

In the first stage, a man turns from darkness to light, from the reign of Satan to God. In the second, he cleanses the dwelling-chamber of his heart from every impurity, in order to receive Christ the Lord, who is coming to him.[15] In the third, the Lord comes, makes His home in the heart of a man and sups with him.[16] This is the state of blessed communion with God—the goal of all ascetic labors and endeavors!

To show the way to salvation means that we must describe all these things and define the rules which govern their operation. Full guidance in this matter takes a man on the crossroads of sin, leads him through the fiery way of cleansing, and raises him up to the highest pitch of spiritual perfection attainable, to the whole measure of the fullness of Christ.[17] In other words, this guidance must show us:

1   how the Christian life begins in us;
2   how it is perfected—that is, how it grows and is strengthened; and
3   how the Christian life appears in its full perfection.

---

15   Cf. 2 Corinthians 7:1
16   Cf. Revelation 3:20. This intimacy with Jesus is a foretaste of the messianic banquet. Very probably, this is a liturgical allusion. Basing their idea on Isaiah 25:6, the Jews often described the joyous messianic era as a banquet. See Matthew 8:11; 22:2–14; 26:29; and the parallels in other Gospels. Also Luke 14:15 and Revelation 19:9.
17   Cf. Ephesians 4:13, *attain to the unity of the faith and of the knowledge of the Son of God, to mature manhood, to the measure of the stature of the fullness of Christ.* Thus, Theophan enjoins upon us the spiritual journey, so that we might attain the goal of the journey, which is to come into our full stature as the adopted children of God.

1

How the Christian Life Begins

The beginning of a grace-given Christian life is established in baptism, but few people preserve this grace for long. Most Christians lose it. In their actual lives, we see that many people are more or less corrupted; they have principles which are not sound, but which were permitted to develop and take root. Others may have good principles, but while still young these people—whether according to their own inclination or because they were seduced by others—forget about these principles and gradually get used to what is harmful. Such people no longer have the true Christian life within themselves; they must begin it anew. Our holy faith offers the Sacrament of Confession for this. *If any one does sin, we have an advocate with the Father, Jesus Christ the righteous* (1 John 2:1). So, if you have sinned, then acknowledge your sin and repent. God will forgive you your sin and put within you *a new heart and a new spirit* (Ezekiel 36:26). There is no other way at all: either do not sin, or repent. Judging from the multitude of those who fall into sin after baptism, one must say that repentance has become for us the only source of true Christian life.

In some people the gift of the grace-filled life, which was already received and acting in them through Baptism, is only cleansed and rekindled by means of the Sacrament of Confession.[1] With others who are more deeply mired in sin, the beginning of this new life is reestablished only through the Sacrament of Confession.

---

1 The Russian word translated as "confession" also means "repentance." Its usage here is clear by the prefacing "Sacrament of." It is important for the English-speaking reader to understand the close connection between these two words in Russian. The Sacrament of Confession in the Orthodox Church is the acknowledgment of one's sins, made by an individual penitent in specific terms to a priest in a private confession, followed by absolution.

We shall begin to consider the Sacrament of Confession from this latter case.

In this latter case, Confession is a radical change for the better, a sudden change of will, a turning away from sin towards God, a rekindling of the fire of fervent desire for the exceptional pleasing of God[2] with the denial of self and all other things. Most of all it is characterized by a painful change of will. A man is accustomed to what is evil; now he must tear himself away from sin. He has offended God; now he must burn in the fire of the incorruptible and impartial judgment of his conscience.[3] A repentant man feels an anguish like that of a woman in childbirth. In the feelings of his heart, he touches to a certain extent the punishments of hell. To a lamenting Jeremiah, God gave the commandment *to destroy* and *to build and plant* anew (Jeremiah 1:10). The lamenting spirit of repentance was sent to the earth by the Lord to pierce those who accept it *to the division of soul and spirit, of joints and marrow* (Hebrews 4:12). This same spirit was sent in order to destroy our old self[4] and lay the foundation for making a new man[5] within us. Within the repenting man there is sometimes a sense of fear, sometimes a slight hope, sometimes a keen sense of his own deep pain, sometimes a slight feeling of consolation. Sometimes he experiences the terrors of near despair; sometimes he feels the gentle breezes of joy and consolation evoking the mercy of God—all in turn. All these feelings make a man feel as if he were a decomposing corpse, as if he were departing from this life, but with the hope of receiving new life.

This state is painful, but salutary. It is so unavoidable that one who has not experienced such a painful change has not yet begun to live through repentance. There is no hope that a man might overcome himself and begin to cleanse himself from all

---

2   This Russian construction is retained in translation because it communicates Theophan's ardor better than a less literal rendering.

3   The Church Fathers say that our conscience is the voice of God within us. Therefore, we cannot bribe this Judge or escape His pronouncements on our behavior.

4   Cf. Romans 6:6, Ephesians 4:22, and Colossians 3:9

5   Cf. Ephesians 2:15

his impurity without having first passed through this furnace of repentance. The resolute, firm, and active resistance to sin can come only from a hatred of sin. Hatred of sin comes from an experience of the harm which is produced by sin. The feeling of harm from sin is experienced in all its might during this painful change through repentance. Only at this point does a man feel with all his heart how great an evil sin is. From henceforth he will flee from sin as from the fires of hell. Although someone may begin to cleanse himself without this painful experience, he will do so only slightly: more outwardly than inwardly, more in his actions than in his inner disposition. Therefore, his heart will still remain unclean, like ore which has not been refined.

Such a change is engendered in a man's heart by divine grace. Only this grace can inspire a man to raise his hand against himself in order to slay himself and sacrifice himself to God. *No one can come to Me unless the Father who sent Me draws him* (John 6:44). God Himself gives a man a new heart and a new spirit (Ezekiel 36:26). A worldly man feels pity for himself; having merged with the flesh and sin, he has become one with them. Only the Supreme Power can divide him into two parts and arm him against himself.[6]

Therefore, the change in a sinner is produced by God's grace; yet it does not occur without the participation of his free will. In Baptism this grace is given at the moment that the Sacrament is completed upon us. In the case of Baptism, free will comes later and assimilates the grace which was given to it. But in repentance, free will must participate in the very act of the change itself.

This change for the better and turning to God must be as if it were instantaneous, and indeed this is so. Although this change is instantaneous, the person passes through several preparatory stages during which his freedom is united with grace.[7] In these stages,

---

6   Theophan's point here is that a man has no power of himself to do this work. Only with the help of God can this work be accomplished.
7   Orthodox theology understands salvation as the result of the interaction of human freedom and God's grace. God extends His saving grace to us, and we are free to accept or reject that grace. The interplay between God and humankind is the subject of this text.

grace gradually takes possession of freedom, while freedom submits itself to grace. These stages are necessary for everyone. Some people pass through them quickly, but for others it takes years. Who can understand everything that is happening here, especially since there are so many ways that grace acts upon us, and the states of people upon which it acts are so innumerable? One must understand, however, that for all this variety, there is one common order of change, and no one can avoid it. Everyone who repents is a person who is living in sin—and every such person is changed by grace. Therefore, based on an understanding of the state of a sinner in general and understanding the relation of freedom to grace, one can depict this process and determine its rules.

2

The State of a Sinner

The sinner who is to be renewed through repentance is often described in the Word of God as being submerged in a deep sleep. The distinctive feature of such persons is not necessarily their manifest depravity. It is rather the absence of an active, heartfelt, and selfless desire for pleasing God, together with a resolute aversion for everything that is sinful. Piety is not the primary object of their concern and labor. They are concerned about many other things, but are absolutely indifferent to the matter of their own salvation and are not aware of the danger they are in. They are neglectful of a good and righteous life, and lead a life that is cold to faith, although this life may sometimes be outwardly irreproachable.

These are the general features characteristic of a sinner. The particular features of a man who has deprived himself of grace are presented as follows. Having turned away from God, a man becomes centered on himself and puts himself as the main object of his entire life and activity. This is certain, because after God there is nothing greater for a man than himself. Having received the fullness of grace previously,[1] and having now become empty without God, he is in a hurry and concerned with how and by what means he can fill this emptiness which is inside of him. This emptiness, which was formed in him as a result of falling away from God, kindles in him an incessant craving that nothing can satisfy.[2] This craving is vague, but constant. A man becomes a bottomless abyss; he tries hard to fill this abyss, but he cannot. That is why for his whole life he is in sweat, toil, and great troubles. He busies

---

1   That is, having received grace in baptism.
2   This emptiness is certainly recognizable in the modern world. Theophan's elegant statement of this emptiness shows his relevance for our time and culture.

himself with various things in hopes of finding satisfaction for this craving that consumes him. These things occupy his entire attention, all his time, and the whole of his activity. They are his highest good, to which he has devoted his whole heart. Hence it is clear why a man who sets himself up as the main object of his life can never be within himself. He is always focused on things outside of himself: on the things which were created or devised as a result of his own vanity in order to fill his craving.[3] He has fallen away from God, who is the fullness of everything. He is empty in himself. The only thing that remains is to spread himself among the endless variety of things and to live through them. So a sinner is thirsty, anxious, and troubled about many and various things which are apart from himself and apart from God. That is why the characteristic feature of a sinful life, when one is neglectful of his salvation, is *an anxiety and trouble about many things* (Luke 10:41).

The nuances and distinctive features of these *troubles about many things* depend upon the kind of emptiness which is formed in the soul. The emptiness of *the mind*—which has forgotten about the One who is everything—gives birth to a concern for excessive knowledge: for much scrutiny, curiosity and inquisitiveness. The emptiness of *the will*—which has deprived itself of the One who is everything—produces numerous desires: striving to possess many things or even all things, so that everything could be in one's own power and according to one's own will. This is the love of worldly possessions.[4] The emptiness of *the heart*—which has deprived itself of real delight in the One who is everything—generates a thirst for many and various false pleasures: the searching and striving for those innumerable things in which one hopes to find sensory

---

3   Theophan distinguishes between those God-given things within a man that can fill this emptiness: *the fruits of the Spirit such as love, joy, peace, patience, kindness, goodness, faithfulness, gentleness, and self-control* (Galatians 5:22), and those created objects that are outside of a man. The outside objects can never fill the inward craving. This distinction is of particular importance in the West, with our intense focus on the acquisition of material objects in our futile attempts to fill our inward emptiness.

4   The Russian word is *liuboimanie*, a technical term used in the Orthodox Church. It refers to covetousness, the striving for possessions, the striving to possess more and more and more. See Luke 12:15.

pleasure, both inwardly and outwardly. So, a sinner persists incessantly in his troubles and anxieties, and in his search for excessive knowledge, many possessions, and diverse pleasures. He is always delighting in outward things, constantly acquiring possessions, scrutinizing things and testing them. He whirls around in this circular process for his entire life. This inquisitiveness attracts and entices the mind; the heart hopes to taste sweet things; and the will is carried away. Anyone can verify this by putting the movements of his soul under his own observation for just a single day.

And a sinner would remain in this ceaseless whirl forever if he were left alone, for such is the nature of our slavery to sin. But this whirling is intensified and complicated a thousand times because the sinner is not alone. There is a whole world full of other people whose main concern is to test and scrutinize, to please themselves, and to possess. These people have justified all these things to themselves. They have put them in a certain order, subjected them to certain rules of propriety, and imposed the necessity of acting in accordance with these rules upon everyone under their dominion. Being connected with each other, these people necessarily come into contact and into conflict. During these frictions, people increase their inquisitiveness, their love for possessions, and their self-indulgence tenfold, a hundredfold, and a thousandfold. People tie all their happiness, bliss, and life to these things.

This *world of vanity*, whose occupations, customs, rules, connections and relationships, language, pleasures, entertainments, and concepts—in short, everything, from things that are small and insignificant to things of great importance—all these things are impregnated with and steeped in the spirit of these children of *troubles about many things* that were mentioned above.[5] They are the cause of the dreary ruin of the spirit in these lovers of this world. Being actively united with this entire world, every sinner

5   The Russian concept is quite clear, but difficult to render into English without a more free translation. The meaning is this: The *trouble about many things,* which is the result of the emptiness we have without God, is the mother. Her children are inquisitiveness, love for worldly possessions, and self-indulgence. Each of these children has its own spirit, which penetrates all human customs, rules, ideas, etc.

falls into its broad nets, wraps himself in them, and is so deeply buried that he cannot be seen. A heavy burden lies upon the sinner, that lover of this world, and on each of his members. He has no power to move or stir, not even a little. He cannot do anything that is not in accordance with the spirit of this world. To do otherwise, he must throw off this impossible load. That is why nobody undertakes this backbreaking work. Nobody even thinks about it! Everybody lives on in the same way, moving along the tracks in which he finds himself.

In addition to this, our trouble is redoubled since there is in this world its own prince, who is the first among all other creatures by reason of his guile and lies, his wickedness, and his experience in seduction. By means of the flesh and materiality, with which the soul has mingled and merged through the Fall, this prince has free access to the soul. He comes to the soul and kindles the fires of inquisitiveness, the love for worldly possessions, and sensual self-indulgence. By different kinds of flattery, he keeps people immersed in these states, hopelessly, constantly, and without any way out. By means of all sorts of promptings he instigates different ideas so that a man may try to satisfy them. Satan then either helps to fulfill these ideas, or else he destroys the man's first plans and suggests new ones which are even more seductive. He does all this with one sole aim—to prolong and deepen a man's staying in these states. All this constitutes a chain of worldly fortunes and misfortunes that is not blessed by God.

This prince has an entire horde of subordinates—the spirits of wickedness.[6] Every moment they rush about through the entire inhabited world in order to sow in one place one kind of seed and in another place another sort. They do this in order to ensnare more deeply those who have already wrapped themselves in the nets of sin, and to repair those fetters which had weakened, become loose, or broken. They do this so that no one will take it into his head to become free from their chains and escape into

---

6   Cf. Ephesians 6:12

freedom. In this latter case, they hastily gather around the willful person. At first they come one by one, then by detachments and then by legions, and finally with their entire horde. They do this under various guises and in different ways in order to block all the exits. In another comparison, they do this in order to push back into the abyss the one who has just begun to crawl up out of it.

In this invisible kingdom there are certain throne-rooms where plans are drawn up, orders given, and reports rendered and received, either with approval or with reproach for the demon who fulfilled his duties. According to the expression of St. John the Theologian, these throne-rooms are *the depths of Satan.*[7] On the earth, in the midst of Satan's kingdom of people, these throne-rooms are as follows: groups of scoundrels, debauchers, and especially groups of blasphemous unbelievers who pour out sinful darkness everywhere by means of their actions, speech, and writing, and through this obstruct God's light. The instrument by which the demons express their will and power in this world is the whole complex aggregate of worldly customs, which are impregnated with and steeped in sinful elements. These worldly customs stupefy a man and seduce him from God.

This is the configuration of the sinful sphere! Every sinner is entirely immersed in this sphere, but he is kept in it by one particular thing. And this *one thing* can sometimes be tolerable in appearance, or even laudable. Satan has one concern: that when a man is completely occupied in his consciousness, his will, and his heart, he is not solely and exclusively devoted to God, but to something that is apart from Him. So, having been joined to these things that are apart from God with his mind, will, and heart, he may have them instead of God and may care only for them, may scrutinize only them, may take delight only in them, and may possess only them. This concerns not only the bodily passions and the passions of the soul, but also the things which are proper and becoming: for example, learning, arts and crafts, and the cares of

---

7   Cf. Revelation 2:24

the day. Everything of this kind can serve as a fetter by means of which Satan keeps blinded and dazzled sinners under his dominion and does not allow them to come to their senses or to collect themselves.

If one looks at a sinner's inward disposition and outward state, then it will be found that sometimes he knows much, but is blind with regards to the works of God and the matters of his salvation. It will be evident that though he is incessantly troubled, he is not active with respect to the establishment of his salvation. Even though he experiences alarm or delight in his heart, he is completely insensitive and dead to everything that is spiritual. In this regard, all the faculties of our being are injured by sin, and a sinner is characterized by blindness, negligence, and deadness. He does not see his state, and that is why he is not aware of the danger of his state. He is not aware of his danger, and that is why he does not care to rid himself of it. It does not even occur to him that he must change and work out his salvation. He is in the firm belief, which nothing can shake, that he is in a good state and on the right way, so he does not wish for anything else, and he works so that everything should remain as it is. That is why he considers any reminder about another way of life as unnecessary for himself. He does not listen to these reminders and cannot even understand what they are for—he avoids and flees from them.

3

The Action of God's Grace

We have already mentioned that a sinner is in the same position as a man who is submerged in deep sleep. Just as one who is in deep sleep cannot awaken by himself and cannot get up if some danger approaches—he needs someone else to come and awaken him—so also one who is submerged in the sleep of sin cannot come to his senses and collect himself. He cannot rise up if God's grace will not come to his assistance. According to God's infinite mercy, His grace is available for everyone. It comes around to everyone and appeals in a distinct way to each person. *Awake, O sleeper, and arise from the dead, and Christ shall give you light* (Ephesians 5:14). This comparison of sinners to those who are asleep gives us certain points for a comprehensive examination of their conversion to God. For example, with one who is asleep: first he wakes up, then he gets up out of bed, and finally he makes up his mind to go do something. So also with a sinner who turns towards God and repents: first *he wakes up* from the sleep of sin, then he comes to some *determination to change* (he is getting up), and finally *he clothes himself* in strength for a new life with the Sacraments of Confession and Eucharist (he is ready to act). In the parable of the prodigal son[1] these moments are indicated in the following way. First, *he came to himself*—this means that he came to his senses and collected himself. Then he said, *I will arise and go*—meaning that he intends to stop his former way of life. Then, *he arose, and went to his father and said, I have sinned*. This is his repentance. And then the father clothed him in his *best robe* (which indicates his absolution) and set the table for him (the Holy Eucharist).

---

1   Luke 15:11–32

So, in the conversion of sinners to God, there are three movements:

1 awakening from the sleep of sin;
2 rising up, with the determination to leave one's sin and dedicate oneself to pleasing God; and
3 the clothing of the sinner with strength from above for this matter of pleasing God in the Sacraments of Confession and Eucharist.

4

Awakening from the Sleep of Sin

The awakening of a sinner is such an action of God's grace in his heart that he, having awakened from sleep, sees his sinfulness and feels his danger. He then begins to fear for himself and concerns himself with how he can rid himself of this trouble and save himself. Formerly he was blind, dead, and careless with respect to his salvation, but now he can see, feel, and care. But this is not the change itself yet. It is only a possibility for this change and a call for it. Here grace just says to a sinner: "See what you have come to. Take care then, and take measures for your salvation." Only grace takes the sinner out of his habitual and customary bondage and relieves him from his fetters. In this way grace affords him an opportunity to choose an entirely new life and to attune himself to it. If he avails himself of this opportunity, then it will be a blessing for him. But if he does not take this opportunity, then he will be submerged again into the same deep sleep as before and will be thrown into the same abyss of destruction.

God's grace achieves this by exposing to the consciousness and feeling of a man the insignificance and dishonor of the things to which he is devoted and which he values so highly. *As the word of God . . . pierces to the division of the soul and the spirit, of joints and marrow* (Hebrews 4:12), so also grace pierces to the division of the heart and sin, and divides their illicit joining and union. We have seen that a sinner in his entire being is falling[1] into a domain where everything—principles, ideas, judgments and opinions, rules, customs, pleasures, orders—is absolutely and completely opposed to the true spiritual life to which a man is destined and called.

---

1   In English, it would be as if the action were completed: the man "had fallen." In Russian, this falling is an endless process, because the pit is bottomless—an interesting and important difference.

13

Having fallen into this domain, he does not stay apart and separate from all these things. He is permeated and steeped with them. He is completely in them, all in all. Thus it is natural for him not to know or think about the existence of things which are opposed to this order, and so he does not feel any sympathy toward them. The spiritual realm is entirely closed to him. Obviously after this, the door to conversion can only be opened on the condition that the order of the spiritual life is revealed to the consciousness of a sinner in all its brightness. And not only revealed; it must also touch his heart. In the same way, the order of the sinful life must also be revealed before his consciousness—and must be repudiated, rejected, and destroyed. Only under these conditions can the desire arise for leaving this sinful order of life and entering into the spiritual order. All this takes place in one act of grace-filled awakening.

In the mode of its action, God's awakening grace[2] always corresponds not only to the kinds of bonds in which a sinner is kept, but also to the special state of a sinner. In this latter case, one must keep in mind the difference in the way grace appears when it acts on those who have never been awakened and when it acts on those who have already experienced this awakening. For the one who has never experienced this awakening, it is given, as it were, free of charge, as a share of the initial, or calling-grace.[3] There is no prerequisite that is required of him because his whole being has been oriented in the wrong direction. But for the one who was already awakened, who knew and experienced what life in Christ was like and who again gave himself over to sin, this awakening is not given free of charge. Something is required from him. He must be worthy and implore God for this grace. He must not only desire

---

2   This is a technical term in Theophan's usage. He differentiates between different kinds of God's grace: the grace of awakening, the grace of attention, the grace of action, the grace of wisdom, and so on.

3   This calling-grace is universal and available to all sinners who have not yet tasted the spiritual life. It is given as a gift for conversion and calls to the sinner. It prepares the sinner for changing his life and gently invites him to turn towards God.

this; he must also act in ways that draw this grace-given awakening to himself. Such a man, remembering his previous Christian life, often wishes to have that life again, but does not receive the power or strength to control himself. He would like to turn over a new leaf, but cannot control or overcome himself. He is in a state of hopeless spiritual weakness. He has been abandoned because he first abandoned the gift.[4] *He has spurned the Son of God, and profaned the blood of the covenant by which he was sanctified, and outraged the Spirit of grace* (Hebrews 10:29). Now he is given to realize that the power of grace is all the greater for the fact that its coming cannot be hastened by him. Seek and labor for it, and through the difficulty of its acquisition, learn to value this grace!

Such a person is always in a painful state. He thirsts, but his thirst is not quenched. He hungers, but his craving is not fed. He seeks, but cannot find. He exerts himself, but does not receive. Some are left in this state for a very, very long time, so that they feel as though they have been repudiated by God, as if God has forgotten, rejected, and cursed them. They are like the land which had drunk the rain that often fell upon it, but remained barren and fruitless (Hebrews 6:7, 8). But this delay of grace in touching the heart of a sinner is only a test. The probationary period will pass and awakening grace will descend upon him again on account of his labor and his hard seeking, while upon some people it descends free of charge.

This course of action of God's saving grace reveals two things to us:

1   the extraordinary actions of God's grace in awakening a sinner, and

2   the usual sequence in acquiring the gift of awakening grace.

---

4   He abandoned the gift of Baptism, and the grace of God which came to him by means of the Sacraments of the Church.

5

The Extraordinary Actions
of God's Grace

It is salutary for the souls of those who live the grace-filled life to know the actions of God's grace, so that—seeing God's great care for sinners—they may glorify the unspeakable grace of God and take heart in the assurance of help from above for every good deed. Those who are seeking God's favor must especially know about and recognize the extraordinary actions of God's grace because in them, more clearly and distinctly than anywhere else, the characteristics of a grace-filled awakening are manifested. We must be fully aware of these characteristics and understand them, so that we can evaluate what we experience. Is it really the grace-given awakening that we experience? And when someone acts, is he acting according to a true grace-given awakening, or according to a self-induced inspiration?

The true Christian life is the grace-given life. Self-made life—however beautiful in appearance it may be and to whatever outward forms of the Christian life it may adhere—can never be Christian. The beginning of the true Christian life is established in a grace-given awakening. The one who responds to this action of grace is not deprived later of the guidance of grace or the communion with this grace during the time that he is faithful to its inspirations. That is why we must make clear to ourselves whether this grace-given awakening has occurred in us. To satisfy this requirement it is possible to say: Judge yourself according to the characteristics of the grace-filled awakening which are revealed in extraordinary cases. These characteristics are the same both in extraordinary cases and in more usual situations. In the former, however, they manifest themselves more brightly and vividly, more definitely and more distinctly.

When a grace-given awakening takes place in the consciousness of a man—as was already indicated—there is an instantaneous destruction of the whole order of his willful and sinful life, and simultaneously the revelation before his consciousness of another divine order which is the one true and spiritually soothing[1] order. Briefly one may depict this order as follows: God, who is worshiped in the Holy Trinity, who created this world, who sustains and providentially cares for it,[2] saves us fallen sinners through the Lord Jesus Christ by the grace of the Holy Spirit, and under the guidance and supervision of the Holy Church. God leads us in the way of the cross, tests us in this life, and brings us to the eternal life of everlasting bliss. This divine order includes and contains all people, events, and institutions, and even the very principles by which everything runs. This entire order, through the action of grace, vividly engraves itself upon the spirit of a sinner.

By contrasting this divine order to everything that he previously lived in and delighted in, the sinner is then obliged to be in absolute accordance and harmony with this divine order. All this strikes him. Every feature of the divine order condemns and rebukes him with his former unreasonableness and carelessness. This impresses him all the more because, at the same time, his spirit sees the obvious insignificance of the former sinful order, which deserves his contempt. By this action the heart is released from

---

1   By *spiritually soothing*, Theophan means that which partakes in the peace of Christ, that which orders the unruly affections and which, by dissolving the self-centered way of thinking, permits the person to enter into his true nature and to return, with the prodigal son, to his Father. This soothing harkens back to the root word *soth*, which means truth. This is the soothing that occurs as one goes back to the Truth, the state of being in the Truth.

2   The Russian phrase, *Bog promishl'aiushii*, which we have translated as "God, who sustains and providentially cares," has a clear and singular meaning in Russian. *Bog* means God. *Bog promishl'aiushii* implies both God's presence and activity in this world. This presence and activity manifests itself by means of His care for this world. It has the meaning that God directs all creation by His gentle care and moves creation towards salvation. He does not deprive the creatures of this world of their freedom, but, by means of His caring and love, draws us into His way, which leads to our salvation.

its former bondage and becomes free. So it is free to choose its new kind of life. This is the limit of the action of a grace-given awakening. It destroys in the consciousness and feeling of a man everything he formerly valued, and vividly shows him what is better. It leaves the stricken and startled man in this state free to choose the new or to revert again to the old. It is remarkable that this grace-given awakening is always accompanied by a startling and by some kind of a fright. This startling and fear occur perhaps because of the suddenness of the awakening. This awakening is like grabbing a sinner at the crossroads of life as if he were a criminal, and placing him before the inexorable judgment of God. Or this startling may take place because the new order which is being revealed to his consciousness is so absolutely new for him and so strikingly opposed to his former order. And this new order is not only new, it is also perfect in all its parts and bliss-giving. In the former state, there is only a sense of sorrow in the heart and the destruction of the spirit.

The starting point for all these salutary actions of a grace-given awakening is a vivid awareness of the new divine order. Proceeding from this notion, let us recall to memory all the recorded experiences of this grace-given action. The consciousness of this new order of being and life is generated in two ways.

1   *Sometimes* this order—in its entirety or in its parts—visibly and perceptibly presents itself in objective reality[3] to the sought-sinner.[4]

2   *But sometimes* the spirit of a man is introduced into this order and he feels it inwardly, within himself.

---

3   That is, the reality of the Divine order is outwardly perceptible by the senses, as in a vision or an apparition, which many see.

4   This is a typical construction in Russian but unusual in English. The Russian language has many words which denote shades of connection between people. This follows from the Russian genius for *community*, which is quite different from the Western genius of individuation and individual development. Theophan makes the point here that the sinner is specially sought out by God.

THE VISIBLE PRESENTATION OF DIVINE REALITY

The merciful Lord reveals to the consciousness of the converting sinner His divine world, in which our spirit is appointed to dwell.

1 *Frequently* He Himself appears for the purpose of conversion in a visible way, taking on some kind of form and appearing either when a man is awake or in his sleep. In such a way He appeared to the Apostle Paul on his way to Damascus,[5] to Constantine the Great, to Eustathius Placidas[6] (September 20), to Neanias who was going to torment the Christians (this is the martyr Procopius, July 8), to Patermuthius in his sleep (July 9), and to many others.

2 *Sometimes* the Lord wishes to send somebody from the other world: either in reality or in dreams, in their own appearance or under some other guise. In such a way the *Mother of God* has appeared many times, either alone, with the Pre-eternal Child, or accompanied by the saints—one, two, or many. The Great Martyr Katherine (November 24), for example, was converted by the appearance in her sleep of the Mother of God with the Pre-eternal Child, who betrothed her to Himself as His bride. Many times *the angels* have appeared, either singly or in assembly. For example, the entire world of the Holy Angels appeared to Blessed Andrew, Fool-for-Christ (November 24), in his sleep, in contrast with the horde of dark powers, which also appeared. Many times *the saints* have appeared; for example, St. Mitrophan appeared to the Lutheran physician, to the sick girl,[7] and to many others.

3 *Sometimes* the other world itself, and particularly its order and main principles, is vividly portrayed in some striking manner

5   Acts 9:1–9
6   The reader is referred to *The Lives of the Saints,* twelve volumes describing the lives of the great souls who have preceded us. The date in parentheses refers to the date of the saint's death, his birthday into eternity.
7   These stories were events of Theophan's time of which his contemporaries would have known.

in the consciousness of a person who is unfamiliar with this order, as in the above-mentioned example of Blessed Andrew, Fool-for-Christ. It is also evident from many other examples in which people who are being converted were shown this divine order in a striking way. For example, the Indian king and his brother were shown a vision of the blessed dwelling places of the righteous. This occurred immediately after the Apostle Thomas (October 6) had given away the money that they had given him to the poor, instead of building a dwelling for himself. In another example, Hesychius the Chorebite (October 3) was shown the terrible torments of sinners. In yet another instance, Peter the Baker, who in great anger threw a loaf of bread at the face of a poor beggar, was shown God's judgment on his actions.[8] Or in other instances, some deep consideration about death and one's subsequent fate were engraved in the minds of Prince Ioasaph (November 19), St. Clement (November 25), and the debauched youth whose dying father requested that he come visit him in his room every evening without fail during his decline.

4   *Sometimes* one is permitted to feel in a palpable way an invisible power which acts amidst the visible powers and phenomena, but which is strikingly different from them and originates from the divine world. Relevant to this point are all the miracles and wonders by the help of which many conversions impossible to enumerate have taken place. The Savior said that unbelievers will not come to believe if they do not see signs.[9] Most of these signs were shown after Christ the Savior by the Apostles during the first years of Christianity, and then, after them, by the holy martyrs. The striking force of the presence of God's invisible power often converted entire villages and towns, and was never without fruit. The blood of martyrs truly lies at the foundations of the Church! *There were also cases*

---

8   That is, God used even this evil deed to turn a man towards the good.
9   Cf. John 20:24–31

where God's power was manifested directly without the mediation of a human person, as when converting Mary of Egypt. This power also manifests itself through the instrumentality of holy things, icons, holy relics,[10] and so on. In this way, the conversion of the Jews in Berothah took place as the result of the miraculous signs which appeared on the icon of the Crucifixion of the Lord.[11] In the moment of all these appearances, consciousness—which has been confused by the different seductions and delusions of this world and which is constantly kept in the visible, sensual, outward order by them—is delivered instantaneously from its bonds and inserted into another order of being and life. This happens by means of a striking, sudden, and immediate appearing to the consciousness of the highest persons and powers, such as Christ, the Virgin, the saints, and the angelic hosts of the invisible realm. The consciousness that has been struck in this way stands in the divine order. Here the same thing occurs as when an object is electrified by a charge from another object. The latter delivers the former from the bonds of matter and, by pulling it to the surface, holds it before itself.[12]

THE INWARD PRESENTATION OF DIVINE REALITY

Our spirit, as we have seen, is closed and stifled by many coverings. But by its nature, the human spirit is a spectator of the divine order. This capacity for contemplation is immediately ready

---

10   In the Catholic and Orthodox Churches there is the tradition of venerating the relics of saints. Certain holy people who have acquired the Holy Spirit in this life have been physically transformed by the Spirit. Their bodies do not decay after death; their remains are sweet-smelling and incorruptible. They are frequently the means by which miracles and healings take place. Literally they are the vehicles of grace from the spiritual realm.

11   This icon of the Crucifixion bled from the wounds of Christ. There have been a large number of miraculous icons throughout the history of Orthodoxy.

12   Here Theophan uses the example of static electricity to illustrate how God's grace brings and holds a person to itself.

to manifest its power, and it really does manifest itself as soon as the obstacles which have bound this capacity are removed. Therefore, in order to awaken the slumbering spirit in a man and to introduce it to contemplation of the divine order, God's grace acts either:

1   *directly* upon the spirit, filling it with strength and power, giving it the opportunity[13] to tear loose from the bonds which bind it, or

2   *indirectly*, as if gradually shaking off these covers and nets from the spirit and by this, giving the human spirit the freedom to be in its own order.[14]

In its direct action, this omnipresent and all-penetrating divine grace invisibly inspires and guides a man's spirit by imprinting on the spirit the thoughts and feelings which separate it from finite and mortal things. This turns the spirit towards the other, better world, though it is invisible and unknown. Common features of these awakenings are *dissatisfaction* with oneself and with everything about oneself, and a vague *sorrow*. A man becomes dissatisfied with everything that is around him. He is not satisfied with his abilities and accomplishments, nor with what he has, even if it were incalculable wealth; and he is as if brokenhearted. Not finding consolation in anything visible, he turns towards the invisible, accepts it with willingness and readiness, and sincerely assimilates it into himself and himself into it.

Many people in this state of dissatisfaction have asked themselves: "What will be the end of all this? And to what result will this bring us?" Then they left everything of their former life. They left not only their old feelings and behavior, but also their entire manner of life. Sometimes there were cases where such dissatisfaction manifested itself primarily in the *sphere of knowledge*. This

---

13   God does not deprive a man of his freedom, but only allows the *opportunity* for a man to choose the life of grace and godliness, or to remain in his former order of life.
14   The natural order of existence for mankind is the divine order. Our natural way of life is to contemplate the Divine, and to stay within the divine order.

occurred with Justin Martyr, who was primarily seeking the light of knowledge of the Divine Being. Sometimes this dissatisfaction manifested itself in the *sphere of the heart,* as with Augustine, who sought most of all a peace for his restless and passionate heart. And sometimes, indeed more often than not, this occurs in the *practical sphere,* in one's *conscience,* as it was with the robbers Moses and David. There were many cases when suddenly the inner dwelling-place of the spirit would be illuminated; the inclination towards the divine world would shoot forth and direct the spirit to some other place. The Lord said about this, *You do not know whence it comes or whither it goes; so it is with every one who is born of the Spirit* (John 3:8).

The spirit often awakens by remembering its previous life as a Christian. In this way were converted Maria, the niece of Abraham the Recluse; the disciple of St. John the Theologian who deviated from the Christian way and was perishing in dissolution; and Theophilus, a church steward. From out of nowhere this remembrance comes within a man and speaks distinctly to the conscience: "Remember from whence you have fallen"—and powerfully strikes the one who has forgotten himself. To this phenomenon one may attribute all conversions that occur after a youthful fall. There can be no doubt that these transformations too are prepared by God's providential care by means of various happenstances which dispose one to accept their grace-filled influence. Therefore, the directness of this impact is only relative. On the other hand, one must also understand that every grace-filled awakening is revealed by similar inclinations and awakenings of our spirit. Through the instrumentality of something visible, grace invisibly and directly touches the spirit, extracts it from its oppressive bonds, and moves it into God's light, into the realm of divine life.

All of the indirect means which refer to this are directed to the destruction of the fetters in which the spirit finds itself. Release your spirit, give freedom to it, and it will flow towards that from which it was taken—towards God. The bonds on the spirit, as we have seen, are thrice-twisted, and are formed by:

1   self-indulgence,[15]
2   the world,[16] and
3   the devil.

Against these three[17] are directed all the destructive actions of spirit-awakening grace.

BREAKING THE FETTERS OF SELF-INDULGENCE

The most immediate fetters on the spirit are those of *self-indulgence* of all kinds, which is a property of our lower animal nature.[18] These bonds of self-indulgence are also the point of contact for other bonds which come from the world and the devil. That is why it is very important to break them, though it is a very difficult and terribly complicated process. Since an unconverted person lives wholly by this lower animal nature, the bonds from this part expand and interlace in a complex manner to the extent that he is submerged in the animal and physical life.

In order to understand how these bonds are destroyed, one must take into consideration that there is *something* [19] with which this animal and physical life joins, on which it feeds, in which it is chiefly manifested, and which forms a solid support for it, providing

---

15   Literally, "self-pleasing" as opposed to "God-pleasing."
16   The following scriptural quotations describe what Theophan means by *the world*: John 8:23; 15:18, 19; 16:33; 17:14–16; 1 Corinthians 3:19; 11:32; Ephesians 2:1–3; James 4:4; 2 Peter 1:4; 1 John 2:15–17; 3:1; 4:4–6.
17   The familiar Western Christian formulation of this is, "the world, the flesh, and the devil."
18   According to Orthodoxy, the animal part of human nature, which is created by God, is essentially good. It consists of our bodily manifestations and was formed by God out of dust in Creation. Prior to the Fall, our animal nature was subordinate to our spiritual nature. This is its proper place. After the Fall, however, this animal part became dominated by the carnal appetites, and so fell into bondage to sin. Thus, our spiritual being became dominated by our carnal appetites. The carnal nature of a man is the seat of his basic physical appetites. When it predominates, there is an absence of an intellectual or moral influence. Christ provides the possibility of redemption from this state by reordering our confused human nature so that the spirit is restored to its dominant role.
19   That is, self-indulgence.

and solidity of its support—rests quietly upon it and, heartily feeding on it, grows and increases with every passing day. The selfishness of a man finds its main food in one mode of self-indulgence, while another man finds it in a different one.

In order to awaken a sinner from his sleep, the divine saving-grace directs all its power towards the destruction of the main support upon which a man rests with all his selfishness. Saving-grace does the following:

- *For the one* who is bound by the indulgence of the flesh, grace plunges him into illness and, enervating the flesh, gives the spirit freedom and strength to come to itself and become sober.
- *For the one* who is fascinated by his own beauty and strength, grace deprives him of this beauty and keeps him in a constant state of exhaustion.
- *For the one* who rests upon his authority and power, grace subjects him to bondage and humiliation.
- *For the one* who greatly relies upon his wealth, it is taken away from him.
- *For the one* who shows off his high knowledge and intelligence, he is disgraced and discredited as naive and unknowing.
- *For the one* who rests upon his valuable connections, they are broken.
- *For the one* who pins his hopes on the "eternity" of the visible order around him, he has this order destroyed by the death of people and the loss of things which are necessary and important to him.
- *For those* who have been kept in the fetters of carelessness by outward happiness and good fortune—by what other means can one sober them if not by sorrows and afflictions? Is it not for this that our entire life is filled with disasters and misfortunes, so that this life might foster God's intention to keep us in inward sobriety?

The destruction of the supports of our careless self-indulgence comprises the turning-points of our life. These destructions act in a striking and salutary way because they are always unexpected.

27

The feeling of fear for one's own life acts most powerfully in this respect. This feeling of fear loosens all the bonds and kills selfishness at its very root; a man does not know where to go. The constriction of life circumstances and the feeling of complete abandonment have the same property as the feeling of fear for one's life. Both leave a man alone with himself, feeling that he is worthless and insignificant. Immediately this sends him up to God, or converts him from self-centeredness to God.

BREAKING THE FETTERS OF THE WORLD

The second kind of bondage is imposed on the spirit by the world, but it lies more superficially than the first. This world—with its ideas, principles, rules, and in general, with all its order, which has been elevated to the status of an unalterable law—lays its heavy, dominating hand upon all its children. Consequently none of them even dares to think about rising up against it or spurning its power and authority. Everybody holds it in reverence, and with some timidity, adheres to its rules. Their breach is considered to be a criminal offense. The world is not a person, but its spirit somehow permeates the earth. This spirit influences us and binds us as with bonds. Obviously its power and authority are created by our thought;[22] they are imaginary, not real or physical. Consequently, we need only to dispel this imaginary authority of the world, and the possibility of sobering from its charms will be near to us.

God's providential care for us acts in four distinct ways to dispel the illusions of this world.

1   God's providential care constantly holds before us two other worlds that are holy and divine. In them and through them, His providential care—exposing these better worlds[23] to our

---

22   According to Theophan, the world is like a hypnotic suggestion: we act as if it is real, but it is not; we act as if it had authority over us, but it does not.

23   These two worlds, visible nature and God's Church, are better than the world mentioned in the paragraph above, which lays its heavy, dominating hand on us.

attention and even allowing us to feel them—speaks incessantly, over and over again, about the emptiness of worldly life and worldly hopes. These worlds are nature,[24] visible around us, and God's Church.

Experience frequently shows that the mind that has been dimmed by worldly fumes becomes sober through contemplation of God's creation, or through entering a church. One man in winter looked at the tree that stood in front of his window and came to himself. Another one, after a noisy conversation, having felt the sweetness of peace of mind that arose while in church, left his former habits and devoted himself to serving God. Visible nature and the Church of God have not only brought to their senses and sobered careless and sinful Christians, but they have even turned pagans towards the true knowledge of God and true worship of Him. For one woman, the word "Hosanna!"[25] sank into her heart and made her Christian. The conversion of our forebears was firmly established once and for all by the influence of the Church upon them. The contemplation of the visible works of God converted the Great Martyr Barbara from idols to God.

The power and influence of these visible works of God depend on the fact that they vividly and tangibly reveal the best and most blissful order of life to a man's spirit that has been weakened, enervated, and exhausted by the vanity of this world. Instantly, pouring into a man the joy and consolation of new life, they bring him to his senses. They give him the understanding that, by giving himself up to the dominion of this world, he only tortures and torments himself. They reveal that happiness is concealed in an entirely different world. They

---

24   For example, Psalm 19:1: *The heavens are telling the glory of God; and the firmament proclaims his handiwork.* Theophan and the Church Fathers understand that nature is fundamentally good. Theophan is distinguishing between three different worlds here: the (illusory) world which lays its heavy hand on us, the world of nature, and the world of God's Holy Church.

25   Which means, in Hebrew, "Save, we pray thee!"

raise the question, if communion with this world is so agonizing now, then what must one expect later? All this gives birth to an inward calling to the divine world and a breaking away from the world of vanity. Sometimes this inward calling and breaking away takes the form of a strong, powerful impulse, but sometimes it is gradual in nature. Ultimately, it wrests the spirit of a man completely away from the fetters of the world. Thus visible nature and the Church press back, drive away, and dispel the charms of this vain and greatly alluring world. For the sake of this, nature and the Church were established by the Lord in such a relationship to us that, by these means, they might act upon us frequently, and even unceasingly, to reveal to us in the most striking way the contrast of one life with another.

2   The second way that grace wrests us away from the bonds of the world consists in this: that by means of the grace of God Almighty, who providentially cares about all creation, a man is presented in reality with a life which is entirely opposed to the one in which he moves. Here especially are referred all conversions that have taken place by means of martyrdom, of which there are innumerable examples. Sometimes the podvig[26] of a martyred one converted entire villages and towns. Here, obviously, is the presence of a moral power from the spiritual world, not from our world. Sometimes it seems that martyrdom must be certain defeat, but this is not so. While being tortured, the martyr remains unconquered and in a good state of mind. It is incomprehensible to man why this is so and how it happens. It is precisely the instantaneous realization of this that flashes through one's mind and dispels the allure of the customs of his former life. This is what happened in the

---

26   The Russian word *podvig* refers to the ascetic labors of a Christian, when a man struggles to go above himself, above his natural powers. *Podvig* is achieved by some kind of sacrifice: of labor, of work, of intellectual abilities, and so on. *Podvig* is inspired by the grace of God. This highly nuanced term is impossible to translate accurately into English using a single word or phrase.

conversion of a robber by King Mauricius, who, instead of putting the robber to death, treated him graciously like an honored person. Also the conversion of a harlot from whom a mother entreated prayers in order to bring back to life her only son who had died. And another harlot came to repentance from observing monks who were humbly engaged in prayer and contemplation of God, while she was luxuriating in sensual pleasure and giving herself up to lewd behavior in the same house.

All the conversions which occurred by means of *examples of someone's life* belong to this category. The power of their action is in the fact that people come face-to-face with those who are satisfied without the usual amusements and reassuring objects. Those who observe also possess many and various kinds of amusements and reassuring objects, but they find neither contentment nor rest in them. From this arises disillusionment and a change of life.

3   The third way of turning souls away from this world is by disgracing the world in the person of its children.[27] Julian the Apostate[28] (A.D. 332–63) exalted himself over everything, ferociously rising against the Christians in his empire. He threatened to suppress them by his power, but then he was killed suddenly and unexpectedly. This not only affirmed those who believed, but also converted many unbelievers to God. In another instance, by reason of false evidence and perjury, an entire village rose up against St. Macarius, beating, torturing, and inflicting punishment upon him. The world appeared to triumph, but then the truth was revealed and it put everyone to shame, returning them to their former veneration and fear of God. All instances of people coming to their senses that

---

27   That is, the children of this world.

28   Julian the Apostate, the Emperor of Rome and a former deacon of the Church, tried to disestablish Christianity in the empire around 361, in order to bring back the pagan religions. His sudden death was taken as a sign that God did not favor his actions. This brought to the faith many who formerly were pagan.

occur through the downfalls and unexpected deaths of the powerful and exalted ones of this world belong to this category. Here the disgracing of the world humiliates it before the face of its followers, exposing its weakness, and by means of this, turns a person away from the world and encourages him to resist and withstand it.

4   Finally, the world itself frequently presses sinners back and drives them away of its own accord, just because it does not satisfy them or because it disappoints their expectations. We are looking for happiness; but in the world there are only fame, honor, power, riches, and amusements—and nothing of this kind satisfies the needs of a seeker. A judicious person quickly notices this deception and comes to his senses. Among the saints of God we see many who, having discerned the vanity and inconstancy of the world, withdrew from it and resolutely devoted themselves to God. In the parable, the prodigal son said, *I perish here with hunger!* (Luke 15:17).

BREAKING THE FETTERS OF THE DEVIL

The third kind of bonds on the human spirit originate from Satan[29] and his spirits. They are invisible and, for the most part, coincide with the bonds of self-indulgence and those of the world. Satan strengthens them by his influence and through them holds the mind in a darkened state. But there is something which has originated directly from Satan. From him comes a vague timidity and fear that troubles the soul of a sinner at all times, and especially whenever he conceives of something good. This is almost the same thing as a master threatening his servant when he is beginning to do something not in accordance with the master's will and plans. From Satan come various different spiritual flatteries and delusions. For some, there is an excessive hope for God's mercy:

---

29   Satan, the proper name of the devil, is variously translated as the Hater, the Accuser. He is an adversary and an opposing spirit.

a hope for mercy that is without true foundation or reason, a hope that is not sobering, but rather deepens the love for sin more and more. For others, on the contrary, it is despair; they are afflicted with doubt and unbelief. In the first instance, it is self-confidence and self-justification that stifle every feeling of repentance.

Yes, many, many things directly depend on Satan, though to define these things is difficult. And yet, one must refer all sinful things to him as their source, for he is the king of the sinful world. One of his cunning ruses is to hide himself; that is, to inspire sinners with the confidence that he does not exist. In consequence of this, he acts willfully and with ferocity in the sinful soul. Satan places sinful aspirations upon human nature. This disposes a man to murmur against God, who allegedly is prohibiting natural things and commanding things to stand which do not, by themselves, have enough power.[30]

Divine grace, which brings a man to reason, frequently extricates sinners from the jaws of hell by shaming Satan. It exposes him to shame and makes him a laughingstock, disclosing his weakness and stupidity and revealing his sly ruses. In this way, Satan was shamed in the person of Simon Magus,[31] in the person of Cyprian of Antioch, and many others. All such occurrences were accompanied by conversions and by the edification of a great number of blinded men. In the days of the Lord Jesus Christ on earth, the demons—the source of unbelief and doubts—became preachers of the faith.[32] The Holy Martyrs, by the power of God Almighty, often compelled both the father and the children of lies to speak the truth through idols in pagan temples.

Such a revelation of the intrigues of the evil one brings a sinner to understand that he is in wicked and hostile hands, that he has been fooled and duped to spite himself. He begins to understand that he has been led along some dark path to ruination, and

---

30 Cf. Genesis 2:15–17; 3:1–7.
31 Cf. Acts 8:9–24
32 Matthew 8:28–32; Acts 16:16–18

those who led him want to rejoice in it. This inevitably gives birth to feelings of danger and fear for one's own welfare. As a consequence, there arise prudence, suspicion, and disgust towards both the cunning one and his inventions; that is, toward the vices and passions and toward the whole of one's former life. From here it is not a long way to the transition that leads to the source of truth, good, and bliss—to God.

ADDING THE WORD OF GOD

Here are the ways and means by which God's grace influences the spirit of a man, delivers it from the bonds which are unnatural for the soul, and face-to-face shows it a different, better life: one in which there is joy and peace. But obviously, all these means in themselves are incomplete; it is as if something is held back. For example, a thirst for that which is better is born—but where is this better life and how does one attain it? Or someone is shaken by fear of death or judgment—but what is one to do in order to avoid this misfortune? It is the same in every case; the answers are not clear. To all of these means must be added one more, which is complementary and consummates the task. This is *the Word,* or preaching.

The Word of God, in its various forms, truly accompanies all the above-mentioned means, elucidating them and indicating their ultimate purpose. Without the Word, these means leave a man still in an uncertain and vague state, and consequently they do not produce everything they are supposed to. For example, the Apostle Paul was brought to his senses by a heavenly appearance,[33] but the Lord had not yet accomplished everything in him. He said, *Enter into the city, and you will be told what you are to do.* Justin Martyr, St. Barbara, St. Joasaph, who was the son of an Indian king, all had seen Satan's lie. But in order to know the truth, they needed special instructors and interpreters. That is why the Lord, who

---

33 Cf. Acts 9:1–5

providentially cares about all creation, has established as law the following: *Go into all the world and preach the gospel to the whole creation*[34] so that *all men everywhere repent* (Acts 17:30). *So faith comes from what is heard, and what is heard comes by the Word of God* (Romans 10:17). This *Word* from the Apostles through their successors is now proclaimed to all the ends of the earth.

There is also an essential need for catechism—for explaining and interpreting the general saving order of God. It is necessary that everyone know the persons and places[35] where one who has awakened from the life of sin can find an explanation, so that he does not lose his awakening, and so that he does not wander about the crossroads exhausting his powers and wasting his time in a fruitless search. The catechetical teaching must be heard incessantly in the church, and indeed it is. The faithful who are present will be edified through this teaching more and more, while the fallen and newly awakened ones will have an immediate guide for the Way that shows things in their true light. How precious the duty of priests to proclaim the saving ways of God both in and out of season, not depending upon the fact that they are generally known. For the most part, this "knowledge" is only presumed![36]

The Word of God not only makes complete all the above-mentioned means, it also replaces them. It awakens a man more fully and more distinctly.[37] By its affinity with our spirit—which also originates from God—the Word of God penetrates within, to the division of soul and spirit.[38] Here it revives the spirit and prepares it to bear fruit with the deeds of a spiritual life. (That is why

---

34   Mark 16:15

35   *Persons* in this sentence refers to the clergy, and *places* refers to the church building.

36   That is, while priests and the public assume that God's saving order is well-known to all, in actual fact it is not.

37   That is, the man is awakened with distinct words and notions that come from Scripture. This is in opposition to a vague, generalized *feeling* about salvation. As Theophan states immediately above, *Without the Word, these means still leave a man in some uncertain and vague state.*

38   Cf. Hebrews 4:12

the Word is called *seed*).[39] Its awakening power is more considerable and substantial because it acts straightaway on the entire man, on his whole composition—on the body, soul, and spirit. A speech sound or the meaningful components of a word strike the hearing. Then a thought occupies the soul, and the invisible energy[40] that is concealed in the Word touches the spirit. If the spirit heeds its call, then—after the Word passes safely through the body and soul, these two coarse tollgates—the spirit awakens. Then the spirit comes into a kind of tension and breaks the bonds which kept it.

The Word of God awakens a man by the most vivid showing forth of the divine order to his consciousness, or by introducing our spirit into this order by destroying the obstacles which keep it from the Divine. For example, one old servant said in simplicity to his sick master, "Fight as you may, sir, there is no getting around death"—and by means of this, awakened the master to repentance. Another man, having read the inscription, "This is what I have done for you; but what have you done for Me?" under an image of the crucified Lord, awakened from his sleep. St. Pelagia heard about the death, judgment, and bitter lot of sinners, and moved away from the sinful life. Holy Equal-to-the-Apostles[41] Great Prince Vladimir was converted by the description of the entire divine order, beginning from the creation of the world to the end of all things, the Last Judgment, and the everlasting lot of those who are good and those who are evil.

In general, the preaching of the Holy Apostles—and following in their steps, all the preachers of the Gospel—consisted in simple representations of the truth, without intellectual elaborations or sophistications.[42] The Holy Apostle Paul says about himself that his preaching was not in the persuasive words of man's

---

39 1 Peter 1:23
40 Alternate rendering: "the energy of life."
41 "Equal-to-the-Apostles" is a title given to Prince Vladimir and to other saints who have been responsible for converting many souls to Christ.
42 In Theophan's time and before, Russian preaching was often quite intellectual and obscure, with multiple literary allusions, allegories, and the like.

wisdom, but in a simple story that told about the matter of salvation through our Lord Jesus Christ, who was crucified on the Cross (1 Corinthians 2:2–4). And this simplicity of preaching, one may say, is the most natural means of influencing a person by the Word. That is, to express the truth as it is, not obstructing it with intellectual understandings and interpretations, and especially not obstructing it with assumptions about probabilities.

The truth is akin to the spirit. Simply and sincerely expressed truth will find the spirit. But the truth that is encircled by images, that is shaped and embellished, will remain in fantasy and imagination. Overloaded with intellectual understandings, interpretations, and proofs, the truth will be detained in the intellect or in the soul, not reaching the spirit and leaving it empty. One may say that the whole matter of fruitless preaching depends upon the over-intellectualized understandings with which one stuffs it. Explain the truth simply; lay bare what it is and the spirit will be conquered. One Jew read the Gospel and converted, for he beheld and felt the truth in the simple Gospel story.

In general, the Word of God, either spoken or written, has directed and converted great numbers of freethinkers to God, by vividly bringing to their awareness the reality of divine things. The truth dispels the darkness of vain thoughts, refreshes the soul, and illuminates the spirit. One may often beneficially employ, in conversations with others, a brief survey of how all things came into being, what will be the end, and why.

On the other hand, obstacles to the spirit are often destroyed by the power of the Word, and freedom is given to it. In this way St. Antony the Great heard the Word about the insignificance of earthly goods and left everything. One youth heard a sermon about the prodigal son and repented. By depicting the vanity of worldly life, many saints succeeded, even on the conjugal bed, in steering their spouses to embrace a pure, unblemished life. In general, both the presentation of the divine order on the one hand, and the exposing of the different worldly charms on the other, fill the soul with the fullness of *saving knowledge,* with a clear and convincing recognition of the saving way. Against this, stubbornness of heart can seldom resist. A great many do not act as they must; that is, with an effort. Instead they remain lost in sleep and carelessness. This happens because they do not know the saving truths, or they know them incompletely. The fullness of knowledge is victorious, for then there is nowhere for the sly and cunning heart to hide.

Because of its universal suitability for awakening sinners, the Word of God goes forth on the earth and reaches our hearing in various diverse forms. It is constantly heard in our churches at every divine service, and at every religious ceremony that is held outside of the church. It is in the chants and hymns of the church. It is in the homilies of the Fathers and in every book which is useful for the soul. It is in those conversations which are salvific for the soul, and in popular edifying sayings.[43] It is in schools, in pictures, and in any visible object which represents spiritual truth. Judging by this, we are enveloped and embraced by the Word of God; we are being catechized from all sides. From everywhere the sounds of trumpets are coming to us for the destruction of the strongholds of sin, as with the walls of Jericho.[44]

In all these ways, the Word of God has already shown—and indeed constantly shows—its victorious power over the heart of man. One must be concerned only that the ways by which the Word of God is dispensed will be observed and guarded, and not interrupted or cut short, so that sincere preaching does not stop, so that the divine service may be performed in good order and for the edification of the people, so that icon painting may be sound and holy, and the chanting sober, simple, and reverent. The responsibility for discharging these duties rests with the ministers of the holy altars. That is why they are the most necessary and most powerful instruments for the conversion of sinners in the hands of

---

43 Theophan is referring to the Russian tradition of embodying wisdom in proverbs and short stories. They are similar to some extent to the apothegms of the Desert Fathers—brief stories which reflect a timeless spiritual wisdom.

44 Joshua 6:1–21

God's Providence. They must recognize and understand this and not keep silence, not only in churches but also in homes, using every opportunity to describe the divine world and to expose the condition of our spirit, which has been seduced by the phantoms of our lower animal nature.[45]

---

45 *Theophan's footnote:* Bishop Tikhon of Zadonsk gave us the most excellent examples of this sort. It seems that he comprehended more deeply than anyone that the best application of the gift of writing and speaking is turning it to awakening sinners from their sleep and bringing them to reason. That is precisely what almost every essay of his leads to. Of the same kind must be every church sermon and every conversation.

the foothold on which it stands. It stands so firmly that it does not fear defeat; it does not even think about it or expect it. For example, when someone has given himself over to[20] the discipline of art, or to worldly matters, or even to learning, and lives in it with all his being, then he is supported by it and rests in it with all his faculties, thoughts, and hopes. Since the entire self-indulgent life which imprisons the spirit proceeds from here, then this support of self-indulgence naturally becomes the foundation for the firmness and solidity of the bonds which are being laid upon the spirit as a result of self-indulgence. This foundation of self-indulgence becomes as it were the point to which all these bonds are attached. Therefore, in order to release the spirit from the bonds of self-indulgence, the divine awakening-grace usually destroys the supports upon which self-indulgent selfness[21] rests. Having shaken these supports at their foundation, grace loosens the fetters and gives to the exhausted and weary spirit an opportunity to hold up its head a little.

There are many supports for our self-indulgence. They are in our being, that is, in our body and soul, in our outward life, and in the whole order of our life. The indulgence of the flesh comes in many different forms. It includes the love of pleasure in food, luxury, lust and carnality, the love for idleness, the passion for amusements, the care and regard for many worldly things, ambition, the love of power, visible success in affairs of all kinds, prosperity, an attractive daily routine, the value of important connections with others, a state of peace in outward relations, passion for artistic skill and beautiful things, for learning, for different activities, and for business. All these modes of self-indulgence, in their many and diverse kinds, form a firm foundation for our selfishness. Our selfishness—with confidence in the trustworthiness

---

20 The verb translated here as *given over to* has the same root in Russian as *passion*.
21 The literal meaning of the Russian is *selfness*. We have retained this meaning in this initial use of the word because the Russian construction gives us an important shade of Theophan's meaning. This word can also be translated as *self-love* or *selfishness*. In subsequent appearances, we typically translate it as *selfishness*.

6

Acquiring the Gift of Awakening Grace

Among the various actions of grace-given awakenings, the usual manner of its action is worthy of particular mention. It employs these actions towards the sinner who has already experienced these awakenings and again has fallen with a sharp tumble into his usual deadly sins.[1] The more frequently these fallings-away repeat themselves, the weaker the awakening becomes, because it is as though the heart gets accustomed to falling. These fallings-away turn into a series of typical occurrences in the natural life. Simultaneously with these diminutions, the grace-filled awakening moves from an energetic feeling—which characterizes its natural state—and approaches more and more the quality of an intention. Finally, it turns into a simple thought or reminiscence. This thought, for the time being, is accepted with consent; afterwards it is only endured—perhaps not with displeasure, but coldly and without particular attention. Then it becomes tiresome and annoying; the sinner hurries somewhat more quickly to be rid of it. Then it is felt with unpleasantness and disgust. Now it is not just disliked, but abhorred. Finally, it is persecuted and driven away.

Accordingly, the conviction that a better spiritual life is necessary diminishes also. At first this necessity presents itself as the only likely possibility. Later it is covered up by doubts in the form of questions about the necessity of a better spiritual life. But later still, its lack of necessity, its superfluity, begins to seem more than likely. Finally the decision is made within a man, "Live as you already live. You may live out your whole life as you already do. All other cares and concerns are superfluous." Here a man comes

---

1 These deadly sins include idolatry, adultery, homosexuality, thievery, greediness, drunkenness; cf. 1 Corinthians 6:9, 10; Romans 6:23.

to the very bottom of evil and negligence. He comes to a condition which is similar to the state of one who has never received an awakening.

Obviously the salvation of such a man is in extreme danger. God's mercy is great, but maybe it will not be able to do anything with him any longer. He is like the land which has drunk the rain that often falls upon it, but does not grow anything; it is a land which is *near to being cursed* (Hebrews 6:7, 8). It is precisely this consequence of not abiding in the spiritual order of life, which is required by the grace-filled awakenings, that must be especially engraved upon the memory of those who need it. True, divine grace is not bound in its actions by such measurings and determinations; yet it happens that it conforms to them. That is why one must not despair of the possibility of conversion and salvation, however faint and weak the calling back to the good life may be. One must, however, with timidity and fear, think about his situation, understanding the current weakness of the invitations of God's grace. Have we not fallen upon the very last opportunity to receive the grace-filled awakening? Have we not blocked all the ways for divine grace, which desires salvation for everyone, to act upon us? Are these not the last approaches to us for the purpose of bringing us to reason and putting an end to the ugliness and disgraceful things of our lives?

Therefore, since such invitations are weak, one must hasten to avail oneself of them with complete steadfastness and strength of intention, and—though this may require more discernment—to intensify them insofar as this is given to the freedom of a man. Obviously, such an effort is nothing other than opening oneself to the grace which is calling and seeking for him. It will truly be an opening, for in our former falls from grace we were coarsening[2] ourselves more and more and closing ourselves to grace, now in one sphere, now in another. This opening will be realized by means

---

2   Throughout this text, Theophan uses the analogy of subtle and coarse when describing the difference between the spiritual world for which we were created, and the world of sin in which we find ourselves.

of entrusting oneself to grace in the way that will now be shown for ascending to the energy of an awakened one. For one must think that this energy will grow simultaneously with the application of this or any other method for awakening and stimulating the sleeping spiritual life in oneself. So while an awakened one fulfills everything with zeal and ardor, quickly and in a fiery way— the affairs of the unawakened go coldly, slowly, and with many difficulties and labors. It is as if grace is leaving him to himself. This gives him a realization of the preciousness of unfailing obedience to God, who calls us, and engenders an inward disposition in him to value God's assistance. When this takes place, the Lord preserves the desire, but the release is not granted at once. He holds a man in the midst of his difficulties—pining indecisively, inclining neither here nor there—in order to test his diligence, and to form and educate his desire and his promise for constancy. Then the Lord unties the one who has been tested.

By these few features we had in mind to distinguish between the two modes of action of God's grace. About one of them the Lord says, *Behold, I stand at the door and knock* (Revelation 3:20), but about the other, *Ask, and it will be given you; seek, and you will find; knock, and it will be opened to you* (Luke 11:9). We have described the first mode. Concerning the second, we will have to address the question: how should we *seek* and on what should we *knock?*

In extraordinary cases the grace of God acts quickly and resolutely, as we see for example with the Apostle Paul, Mary of Egypt, and with others. But in the ordinary sequence of conversion, for the most part it happens in the following manner: that only the thought or the intention comes[3] to a man—to change his life and rectify his deeds and inward dispositions. The thought or the intention comes—but how much one must strengthen it so that it might overcome and subdue the soul! For the most part, good

---

3   That is, God's grace gives the thought to the person. In this sense, the thought has an existence that is independent of the thinker, since it originates from God. The thought is received by the man, and has an affinity with his deepest nature.

thoughts and intentions of this kind remain fruitless and unavailing. This is through no fault of their own, however, but through an improper attitude towards them by those whose soul they visit.

DRIVE AWAY PROCRASTINATION

The first and principal error with respect to these thoughts and intentions is that they are left unfulfilled; their fulfillment is postponed with every passing day. The postponement of conversion is a common affliction and the first cause for incorrigibility. Everyone says, "I still have time," and remains in the usual habits of his ordinary evil life. So when a good intention to change yourself comes, catch hold of it; devote yourself to this matter for the sake of your salvation. And with this purpose, first and foremost drive away this procrastination.

Drive away procrastination. Do not permit yourself to say, "Tomorrow, or sometime later I will busy myself with this," but immediately set to work and begin. Take sound reasoning[4] as an instrument for yourself, and with its help:

1 Imagine more vividly and quickly the ugliness and peril of procrastination. You say, "Later!" But later it will be more difficult to do this, because you yourself will be more accustomed to sin and sinful circumstances, and connections will become more intricate and tangled. What is the sense in one who is already entangled entangling himself more and more, thinking that later it will be as easy for him to get disentangled as it is now? If you truly realize this, you cannot continue in the same way as you are now. Why then delay? You see, ultimately God may say, *I am weary of carrying you* (Isaiah 1:14),[5] and

---

4   Reasoning is a technical spiritual term. It refers to that faculty that uses sense-data to produce concepts, logically order them, and draw inferences or conclusions from them. It produces knowledge that is of a lower order than spiritual knowledge, which comes directly from God.

5   In the Russian facsimile of Theophan's text, there is included what appears to be a further quotation from Isaiah, "You were in satiation for Me." This quotation does not exist in Isaiah 1:14. This apparent mistake may be the result of a corrupted translation of the biblical text from which Theophan was working.

you yourself may also overstep a boundary beyond which there is no return. To avoid misfortune of this kind, there is no labor that one might reasonably regret.[6] If conscientious thought attends to this matter and pictures all these consequences distinctly and vividly, then all the main functions of the soul will avert themselves from procrastination and there will be no defender for this postponement within. You will see that procrastination itself treats you in a hostile fashion, and you yourself will come to look at it with animosity.

2 We procrastinate because a good thought that has visited us stands in us for the time being only as a thought; it has not yet drawn our sympathy or set our desire in motion. Among our other interests it appears as an alien visitor. It beckons from afar, but does not produce much of an impression. It is your work now to take it further into the depths of the soul and to point out its value and attractiveness. So, put it first and foremost in your mind, imagine its rightness, envision the gladness of its promises, picture the heights to which it draws you, assure yourself of the ease of its fulfillment. The good thought acts feebly and does not attract the heart because there are other designs in mind. There are things that seem more interesting, as pointed out by the inclinations that have occupied you before. So, call them all together and compare them impartially. Nothing can compare with what the good intention offers; every other thing which has occupied your mind will be pushed far away. Only that which is being shown by the good intention will remain, and it will draw you to itself as the only valuable and beautiful thing.

3 We suffer from the plague of procrastination mostly because we allow the energy which is within us to weaken. We indulge in laziness, listlessness, sleepiness, and indecision, both in our thoughts and in our actions. You can work on yourself from this perspective too. Vividly imagine how humiliating and degrading it is to permit these things in ordinary actions, and

6   That is, no labor is too much to avert this misfortune.

then imagine how much more degrading this is in the most necessary matter of your salvation. In everything you must be lively, quick, and energetic. It is a shame to permit the opposite. It is a shame to postpone until tomorrow what you can and must do today.

By these and similar methods, drive away procrastination. However you might be able to do this, just do it. A good thought comes. Persuade yourself not to postpone its fulfillment; dispose yourself and make yourself begin to act immediately, according to its indications. For the one who has postponed the matter until the next day, it is of no use to offer any further counsel.

But let us suppose that a good thought is accepted and occupies one's attention. Now you must hasten to bring it to such a level of awakening that it is strong enough to become the lever by which all that is within you may easily and energetically be put into motion. For this you must give space for it to pass inside—and you must do certain, let us call them "operations" with yourself as the most necessary and efficacious preparation for this awakening.

These operations must be opposed to those subtle nets, to that ordering of the inward dispositions that holds a man in sin. Sin entangles the soul with many nets. It conceals itself from the soul by many coverings, because by itself it is hideous and deformed and on first sight, might push a person away from itself. The deepest cover, and that which is closest to the heart, is composed of *self-delusion, deadness,* and *carelessness.* Higher and closer to the surface there are *distractions* and *anxieties about a multitude of things.* These are the principal actors which conceal and feed sin, sinful customs, and the sinful order of life. The uppermost covering—this is the *prevalence of the flesh*—is the cover which is more visible than the others. It is, however, no less powerful and substantial.[7]

7   These coverings correspond to the bonds on the spirit mentioned above in Chapter 5. The uppermost covering corresponds to self-indulgence, the middle covering to the world, and the deepest covering to the devil.

The first cover—self-delusion, deadness, and carelessness—is the essential cover. Its effect is that a man does not see the danger of his state and does not desire to change it. The last two covers are merely instruments; by their means the sinful state is simply manifested and maintained. When divine grace comes, it pierces to the division of *soul and spirit,*[8] strikes straight at the first cover, and tears it off. Under its action a sinner is instantly exposed and stands before his own consciousness in all his ugliness and deformity. But when a man seeks the grace-filled awakening by himself alone, he must begin to act from without and thread his way within.

---

8   Cf. Hebrews 4:12

7

Removing the Coverings of Sin

If you truly want to devote yourself in the proper manner to the intention which preoccupies you—that of transforming your evil life—begin to take off the sinful coverings as one would remove layers of dirt in order to uncover that which is concealed there.

BEGIN WITH THE BODY

Begin first with the *body*.[1] Deny your body pleasures and enjoyments, restrain the satisfaction of your most natural physical necessities, extend the hours of your vigil, reduce your usual measure of food, add to your labors with new labors. The main thing—as you desire and as you are able—is to lighten the flesh, wear away its corpulence.[2] By this means, the soul will disengage itself from its binding by the flesh, will become more lively and active, lighter, and more receptive to good impressions. The material body, prevailing over the soul, imparts its immobility and coldness to it. Bodily labors loosen these bonds and remove their consequences. True, not every sinner lives intemperately and indulges the body. But scarcely will be found a person among those who live a usual and ordinary life who has nothing to deny his body when the longing for salvation sinks into his heart. And the purpose signifies much;[3] it totally and completely changes your actions. What

---

1 That is, bodily discipline will dissolve the bond or covering of self-indulgence.

2 Alternate renderings: coarseness and crudeness, stoutness. The term refers to those coarse qualities which keep the person from apprehending and responding to the spiritual world.

3 That is, the purpose of a bodily labor determines the spiritual outcome of that labor. One might, for example, become a vegetarian for the sake of one's health. This will not have a spiritual result. On the other hand, if one deliberately refrains from meat-eating as a spiritual fasting, this will have a spiritual result. The intention controls the outcome.

you did before according to custom, or in favor of your own duties, now begin to do—of course, with some changes and additions of austerity—for the sake of your salvation, and then you will tangibly feel the difference.

WORLDLY CARES AND DISTRACTIONS

The body burdens the soul from outside; *worldly cares* and the *distraction of thoughts*[4] torment and exhaust it from within. Let us assume that the flesh is already restrained; by this the first step is done. But two more tollgates separate the soul from itself.

Worldly cares do not leave a man time to take care of himself. With them there is one business in the hand and dozens in the head. That is why worldly cares drive a man on and on all the time, leaving him no opportunity to reflect upon his situation. So put aside for a time all worldly cares without exception. Put them aside only for a time. Later you can take up your usual activities in their due course, but for the time being, stop. Release them with your hands, put them out of your mind. But even then, when worldly cares and activities have ceased, confusion will remain for a long time in the head. Thoughts race through one after another; sometimes they are in accord with each other and sometimes they contradict one another. The soul is distracted; the mind sometimes leans one way and sometimes another. By this means, the mind does not allow the establishment of anything permanent and firm in itself. So, gather your scattered children together into one—as a shepherd gathers his flock, or as a magnifying glass gathers the dispersed rays of the sun—and direct them inward.

The desire to go deeply within yourself, to devote attention to yourself, and to cut off distracting thoughts and worldly cares will certainly demand—as their inevitable means—solitude on the one hand, and on the other the cessation of ordinary activities, both those of everyday life and official ones. And the above-mentioned

4   Worldly cares and distractions are the fetters imposed on the spirit by this world.

subduing of flesh will require a change in the way you satisfy your natural physical necessities. Judging from this, you must consider that the most opportune time for establishing this change of life is the time of some fast, and especially the time of Great Lent. Here everything is predisposed to this change—at home, in church, and even in society. That is, everyone looks at this time as a period of preparation for repentance and confession. However, it does not follow from this that when a good intention about changing one's life comes, that you should postpone the fulfillment of this until the beginning of a fast. Everything that is required for this change can also be accomplished at any other time besides a fast. But of course, when a holy fast comes, it is a sin not to take advantage of it for the salvation of the soul, as we miss other times for this. For the one to whom a saving intention about changing his life comes, but not at the time of a fast, and who finds obstacles in his everyday life for putting the intention into practice—then it is best for him to withdraw for a time to a monastery. There the circumstances will be more favorable for one to overcome himself.

THE PROCESS OF AWAKENING

Look, you are standing at your heart now. Before you is your inward man,[5] who is submerged in the deep sleep of carelessness, deadness, and blindness. Begin to awaken him. The good intention which has come is already disturbing him a little. Therefore, begin with more assurance and with the most powerful and intense force of thought. Having gathered together all your attention, begin to direct at yourself ideas of different kinds which are compelling and powerful, and apply them to your inward state.

REMOVE THE COVERINGS
First of all, remove from the eyes of your mind the coverings which are keeping it *in blindness.* If a man does not leave sin and flee from it, this is because he does not know himself and the danger

---

5   Cf. Romans 7:22; Ephesians 3:16

in which he lingers for the sake of sin. If his eyes were opened, he would flee from sin as one flies from a house which is enveloped in flames. Such blindness is a result of a lack of attention to oneself. A man does not know himself because he has never entered into himself and has never reflected upon himself and his moral state. For the most part, this blindness is maintained by certain prejudices about himself. A man by himself forms a network of prejudicial thoughts, which systematically close him off from himself. Even if these thoughts are like a cobweb, composed of only the most tenuous probabilities, the mind has no time to investigate or understand them. And here there is, in addition, the heart,[6] which speaks so loudly for their reality and truth. These are, strictly speaking, our moral delusions or prejudices which arise from the interference of the heart in the business of the mind.[7] That is why, from this moment, you must join to deep attention a certain inward sobriety that pushes aside every flattery of the cunning heart. From this minute, if the heart needs to feel something, let it feel under the influence of ideas of the mind and not by itself, as though it were running ahead of the mind. Otherwise it will again force the mind to imagine things in its own way; again it will subordinate the mind to itself; again it will bring forth disorder in your ideas, and instead of clarifying, it will plunge you into a still more blinded state.

Now having put yourself in such a position, begin to examine the different thoughts which are keeping you in your blinded state. Subject them to a strict and impartial judgment.

1   *"I am Christian,"* you say, and you settle and rest on this. Here is the first flattery—transferring to yourself the privileges and promises of a Christian without taking care to root yourself in

---

6   Here Theophan is talking about the lower, carnal aspect of the heart—unrestrained feelings. This is qualitatively different from the deeper or higher aspects of the heart. Theophan's idea is that having a *feeling* about something does not make it true. You need to check this feeling against the best understanding of the intellect, which is the higher aspect of the heart.

7   Rationally one might know that an action was morally wrong, but the lower carnal part of the heart might persuade one that it was acceptable.

true Christianity; or appropriating the name of what can only be sustained by force[8] and by inner dignity. Explain to yourself that hoping for the name is deceptive; that God is able from these stones to raise up children for Abraham[9] and at any time He can revoke His promises, as soon as the conditions for partaking in them are not fulfilled. The main thing is this: make clear to yourself what it means to be a Christian, carefully compare yourself to this ideal. Then you will see just how well-grounded is this support of your blinded state.

2   *"Surely, you know, we are not worse than others."* We do know something. And if we want to begin to discuss something, we are able to do so. Moreover, we run our affairs and our business not in a random manner or without order, as others do. In this way some people are tempted by their intellectual perfections. Others, on the contrary, are dazzled by their physical perfections: their strength, beauty, or family of origin. Both kinds of people are more sharply dazzled the higher they stand over everyone in their surroundings. Convince yourself:

a   That natural perfections have no moral value at all, because they are not our acquisition, but are given to us by God; especially since, in the Christian understanding, all natural things are worthless because of the damage to our nature in the Fall. Sanctify the good[10] in you by faith in Christ the Savior and by living in accordance with this faith, and then look at it as you would look at true good.[11]

---

8   Cf. Matthew 11:12. That is, only through repentance and *podvig,* both of which involve force, can one in fact become a true Christian.

9   Cf. Matthew 3:8, 9

10   Here, Theophan means both the good within you, and the good that is expressed in your deeds.

11   That is, when your good is sanctified by faith in Christ, it becomes true good. Theophan's understanding here is quite opposed to the contemporary view. The contemporary view believes that human beings are good in their nature. This view, however, is greatly mistaken. This so-called good nature of humankind has led to innumerable wars, genocide, torture, moral corruption, and so on. The twentieth century has certainly seen enough contrary evidence of this to be convincing. Yet the delusion persists. The nature of our fallen state is best understood by the *(cont.)*

b Again, have you done everything that you can and must do according to your talents?[12] More will be required of you if you were given more.[13] The matter is not about abilities and talents, but about their usage. Show what you have gained by them! Do the profits correspond to the amount that was invested?

c There is nothing to say regarding physical advantages or any sort of accidental advantages. St. John Chrysostom in one of his homilies describes a man who praises another for his good looks, his stately manner, his wealth, that he has a lovely house, rides on wonderfully adorned horses, and so on. Afterwards St. Chrysostom addressed the speaker and asked, "Why did you not tell me anything about this man himself? Nothing that you told me is about the man himself."[14]

d And there is no need to look at others; let them be by themselves. *So shall each of us give an account of himself to God.*[15] You look at yourself, and having separated yourself from others, judge only yourself without comparison to others. Or, if you really want to compare yourself with someone, then compare yourself to the saints who have pleased God. They are the living Christian law, and the living models of those who are working out their salvation. If you begin to judge yourself by them, you will not make a mistake.

3 *"We are not really that evil."* It seems as though we do not behave disgracefully, and others do not view us as people who are bad or vile. They do not deprive us of their respect and attention; and besides, these are not just ordinary people, but

---

(cont.) traditional Christian understanding: that humanity has fallen and been thoroughly corrupted. This state is remedied only through faith in Christ, and life according to His commandments.

12 Cf. Matthew 25:14–30
13 Cf. Luke 12:48
14 That is, only the outward trappings were described, nothing of the man himself.
15 Cf. Romans 14:12

also persons of high rank. A covering of the thickest darkness is blinding you by means of decency in outward conduct and outward relations! Make clear and impress upon yourself that the outside is not valuable without the inside.[16] Outward correctness and decency in conduct are the leaves, whereas the inward good dispositions are the fruit. By its leaves a fig tree promised fruit, but the Savior, having not found fruit on it, cursed it. Everyone who is outwardly decent and correct, but without a truly good and God-fearing heart, is just the same as this fig tree before the Lord. *My son, give me your heart,*[17] says the Lord in the Book of the Wise. Out of the heart come all good and all evil.[18] What you are in your heart, such you are before the face of the Lord. If you are proud in your heart, then however much you may show your outward humility, the Lord will see you as proud.

Everything is like this.[19] The judgments and opinions of others are deceptive flattery. Others do not know you, but treat you kindly, either supposing you to be good or submitting to the rules of propriety. Does it not happen that those who are near us see the evil in us, but do not speak to us about it for their own reasons? Does it not also happen that some, seeing evil in others, praise them for that, and by this excite and inspire a certain spirit of foolhardiness in doing evil? And the injudicious listener plunges forward deeper and deeper into evil and into bad deeds. For when a man sees happy smiles upon the faces of people around him as a result of his actions, then he remains in evil with a certain self-satisfaction and smugness. There is danger lest we too suffer something similar to this, if we listen so keenly only to the opinions of others!

---

16 Cf. Matthew 23:25–28
17 Proverbs 23:26
18 Cf. Luke 6:45
19 That is, the Lord sees what is within the heart and, whether it is pride, greed, lust, or any other passion, the Lord will judge accordingly, despite all outward signs to the contrary.

4   But even when we acknowledge that there is bad in ourselves, we blind ourselves by the ordinariness of sin around us. We ask, *"Am I the only one?* This one is like me, and that one, and look, even this one. And are there not many like this who are evil, even worse than I am?"* Make clear to yourself that great multitudes of those who commit sin do not change the truth of the law. They deliver no one from responsibility. God does not look at number. Even if all will sin, He will punish everyone. How many people were born before the Flood, but all perished except eight souls.[20] And together with Sodom and Gomorrah, five cities were consumed by fire from heaven, and no one escaped except Lot with his daughters.[21] And in hell, the torments will not be easier because many find themselves there. On the contrary, will not the sufferings of everyone become more anguished because of this?

By these and similar reflections, hurry to dispel the darkness of prejudicial thoughts that are keeping you in blindness and not allowing you to look at yourself properly. Make it the aim of this first work on yourself to bring yourself to doubt and hesitation concerning the safety and security of your standing. You will reach this naturally when you begin to take away, one after another, the supports on which your blindness falsely strengthens itself; when you, little by little, begin to destroy those vain and empty hopes about yourself and the things that are yours; when little by little you begin to smash the excuses for your *wicked deeds*—that is, the inclination always and in everything to justify yourself and to make excuses. Convince yourself that your Christianity leads to nothing if you are bad; that your perfections more convict you than excuse you; that your outward decency is hypocrisy, which is hated by God while your heart is uncorrected and uncleansed; that neither the praises of others nor the vastness of fellowship in wrongdoing will shelter you from the judgment and wrath of God. Little by little you will stand apart in your thoughts and become alone—

---

20   Cf. Genesis 6:10; 7:1–7
21   Cf. Genesis 19:24–30

alone before the gaze of your mind and conscience, which will give a strong voice against you. Particularly after you have compared yourself with that which it is necessary for you to be in Christ, you will find that you are far from your Prototype.[22] In consequence of this—if your consciousness will not be cunning and lie to itself—it will be natural for you to become frightened for yourself. Being cut off as it were from everyone and being deprived of all supports, you must be astonished by the feeling of hopelessness and apprehension for yourself. In every way possible you must bring the above-mentioned work on your blindness to this very limit. The revival of this feeling[23] is always the threshold for the flight of sin, just as in a battle a wavering in enemy ranks is a sign that they will soon be put to flight.

GO EVEN MORE DEEPLY INTO YOURSELF

Second, as soon as you feel the slightest sense of your sinfulness and the danger of remaining in it, go even more deeply into yourself, and with still greater force of thought, strike yourself with a formidable and sobering presentation. By this means, shake and soften your *dead heart,* as a heavy hammer softens hard stone.[24]

1   Bring to mind your last hour. Say to yourself, "Alas, *my death is soon.*" One after another are dying around you, and your hour too is just about to strike. Not removing yourself from the hour of your death,[25] impress on yourself that the angel of death has already been sent, is coming, and now draws near. Or imagine yourself as a man over whose head a sword is ready to strike. Then imagine even more vividly what will happen to you in dying and after death. *Behold, Judgment is standing at the doors.*[26] Your secrets will be exposed[27] before the angels and

---

22   Our prototype is Adam before the Fall; cf. Genesis 1:26, 27.

23   This is the feeling a person has prior to falling into sin. Now the feeling is revived by the grace of God and with the cooperation of one's own efforts.

24   Cf. Ezekiel 11:19–21

25   That is, live with the constant awareness that your death is imminent. This is particularly important in a culture like our own that denies death, and whose members constantly believe that their own death is in the distant future.

26   Cf. James 5:9   27   Cf. Romans 2:16

all the saints. There before the face of everyone you will stand alone with your deeds. From them you will be either condemned or justified.[28] But what is *paradise* and what is *hell?* In paradise there is bliss that cannot be described. In hell there is torment without consolation or end; and on hell there is the stamp of God's resolute rejection and repudiation.[29] Receive and instill all this in your heart and compel[30] yourself to dwell in it until *dread and terror* fill you.

2   Then turn to God and place yourself—you who are defiled and burdened with many sins—before the face of Him who is omnipresent, omniscient, all-gracious, patient and slow to anger! Will you still offend the eye of God by your loathsome and sinful appearance? Will you still ungratefully turn your back upon the One who is gracious to you in everything? Will you still stop up your ears against the fatherly voice that is mercifully calling you? Will you still push away the hand that is being extended to accept and receive you? Understand and receive in your heart this discrepancy, and hurry to arouse and strengthen in yourself *godly grief and sorrow.*[31]

3   Besides, remember that you are Christian, that you have been redeemed through His blood,[32] that you have been washed in the water of Baptism,[33] that you have received the gift of the Holy Spirit,[34] that you partake of the Table of the Lord and feed on His Body and Blood.[35] And all this you have trampled underfoot[36] for the sake of the sin which is destroying you!

28   Cf. Romans 2:6–8
29   For those who consistently reject God, God finally will disown them.
30   *Compel* is a variant of a technical term which we often have translated as "force"; it is a kind of self-coercion. In spiritual matters, this is like taking a foul-tasting medicine. While it is unpleasant for a time, it will restore you to health. In the same way, the spiritual disciplines, which are unnatural to our fallen natures, are necessary for the well-being of our soul.
31   Cf. 2 Corinthians 7:10
32   Cf. Ephesians 1:7
33   Cf. 1 Corinthians 6:11
34   Cf. Acts 2:38
35   Cf. John 6:53–58
36   Cf. Hebrews 10:29

Ascend in your thoughts to Calvary and realize how much your sins cost . . . Is it possible that you will wound the head of the Lord again with the crown of thorns of your sins? Will you again nail Him to the Cross, pierce His side, and mock His long-suffering patience? Or did you not know that in sinning you participate in tormenting the Savior and will share the fate of His tormentors? But if you cease your sin and repent, then you will share in the power of His death.[37] Choose one or the other: either crucify Christ and perish eternally, or be crucified together with Christ and share eternal life with Him.[38]

4   Reason further: what is this sin to which you are nestling so closely? This is the evil which is the most calamitous of all evils. It estranges us from God; it disorders and ruins our soul and body; it hands us over to the torments of our conscience; it subjects us to the tortures of God during this life and in the time of death; and after death it plunges us into hell, closing paradise forever. What a monster we cling to! Understand in your heart all the evil that comes from sin, and exert yourself *to detest it and abhor it.*[39]

5   Finally, consider sin from the perspective of the devil, its originator and multiplier, and see for whom you are working by means of your sin. God did and is doing everything for you, but you do not want to please Him. The devil does nothing for you except tyrannize you by means of sin, and yet you willingly and untiringly work for him. You befriend him through your sin, but he bears malice to you through it. He beckons you to sin by promising sweetness from it, but those who fall into sin he torments and tears apart by this same sin. Here he suggests that sins are nothing, but there he will bring them against you as the important points at your judgment. He shakes with malicious joy when someone is caught and remains in the nets of sin. Consider all this and stir up in

---

37 Cf. Romans 6:5–11
38 Cf. Galatians 2:20
39 Cf. Deuteronomy 7:26

yourself an enmity towards this hater of mankind and towards his deeds.

So when you squeeze into your heart, one after another, these feelings and understandings which break and soften the heart[40]— now with terror and dread, at another moment with grief and pity, at another with loathing and hatred—then little by little your heart will grow warm and come into action. And following the heart, your enervated will also begins to come into motion and tense itself. As streams of electricity impart to a substance a certain tension and activation, or as the brisk morning air imparts a certain freshness and mobility to a man, so also these feelings, having filled the soul, will awaken and stir up the soul's sleeping energy and will revive the impulse and readiness to act for the purpose of leaving this dangerous state. This will be the first fruit of active care for your salvation. So from this minute, hurry along even more resolutely.

DRIVE AWAY CARELESSNESS

Third, drive away the slumber of carelessness. The will for doing good is weakened by lingering in sin. Now, gather around the will those thoughts which awaken its energy. On the side of good, imagine its saving power, its height, its suitability for everything, its ease of fulfillment and ability to overcome obstacles, its joy and consolation, which are always ready, and the chief thing, its necessity. On the side of sin, imagine everything that is opposed to this. Impress these things upon yourself and sincerely ponder them for a long time, until you rouse and motivate yourself and bring yourself to a vigorous tension, instantly ready to set to work. Say to your soul:

1   Well then, you have one of two choices: either perish eternally if you remain in sin, or repent, turn to the Lord, and keep His commandments. So why delay? The more you procrastinate, the worse it gets. Besides, be on your guard and understand that death is at the door.

---

40   Cf. Psalm 51:17

2   Is it really so much work? Just make the first step and take up these labors.[41] The Lord is near and is ready to give you every help.

3   What a blessing! If you will throw off the burden of these bonds, you will enter into the glorious freedom of the children of God.

4   Why do you torment yourself as if you were an enemy? You have no peace day or night. Everywhere there is disarray and anxiety. Make just one change within yourself and all this will disappear; you will see joy and the consolation of life.

5   Look, all are already making their way to the Lord . . . this one is converted, and another, and a third. Why are you standing still? Go! Are you any worse than the rest?

6   Everything around you lives an abundant life and constantly calls you to this life. God is not the God of the dead, but of the living.[42] So join those who live His life. Go and drink from the springs of living water.[43]

The energy of a weakened will is always awakened and aroused when a man places himself between the extremes—either perish or reform your life. When you do this, the instinct for self-preservation will immediately awaken you to action. After this, remember what a great blessing is in store as a result of changing your life for the better. Remember how easy it is to do this, and how able you are to do this. Understand that you are called to this new life and that you have every means for it ready at hand. See how all the righteous ones on earth and in heaven will be gladdened. They will enter into communion with you; they will take you in their arms and the joy of our common life with all who live in Christ Jesus our Lord will begin in you. Show yourself all this and your exhausted will shall awaken, and your weakened knees shall be straightened.

---

41   This verb has the same root as *podvig*, and indicates here the need for bodily labors.

42   Cf. Luke 20:38

43   Cf. John 4:10, 14

8

The Use of Reasoning
in Drawing Closer to God

Working on yourself in this way, you will more and more drive away your blindness, deadness, and carelessness. But work, and work without slacking. There is a slyness and deceit in the sinful soul. The soul in this state evades in every way possible the work which pertains to salvation. Come, take the soul and carry it; it will not object—it just does not want to work by itself. No one can be master of your inner life except you yourself. Enter within yourself and strike yourself, break yourself, and bring yourself to reason. Deal with yourself before the face of God; keep persuading and convincing yourself. In the matter of conversion, reasoning with yourself is the only door for this. After all, if you will not think through and ponder what is to be done, then who will do this for you? That is why it was said to you above: "Carefully consider and think through this, imagine that, thoroughly scrutinize these other things," and so on.

What a great blessing it is for a sinner if his depravity has not yet had time to extinguish the light of the knowledge of the truth within him. Let his inward disposition be corrupt, let his feelings be unclean, but if *sound ideas* are kept and preserved in the mind, then there still is something on which the man who has begun to think about his salvation can gain a toehold. But when there are no sound ideas, when the mind has become corrupted as well, either it will fall into doubts, having lost conviction, or it will accept distorted and perverted teachings. Then there will no longer be any point of leverage from which a man can act on himself. Then one has to accept that *from the sole of the foot even to the head there is nothing sound in it, only bruises, welts, and raw wounds, not pressed out or bandaged, not softened with oil;*[1] that from the foot to the head, there is no wholeness in him. Few are reduced to this state, however. And those who are reduced to such a state—if conversion is possible for them—are converted by the extraordinary and striking action of God's grace.

But most sinners do not lose their faith, or according to the Apostle, *the pattern of sound teaching;*[2] they only become morally corrupted. For such people it is enough to cleanse the thoughts which were darkened by forgetfulness, and to restore their weakened conviction, which arose from negligence and lack of attention towards every good. Sit, and by yourself scrutinize everything: what you must believe, how to live, and what to expect—according to the Creed of the Orthodox faith and the commandments of the Lord. If you find this difficult, then look in the Catechism. If you cannot even do this, then talk with someone; it would be best to speak most intimately with your spiritual father.[3]

When you do this, the sovereign truth will arise victorious within you. With authority and power, it will start to press back the wrongness of your actions, your inward dispositions, and the feelings which have taken possession of you. Then it will be easy for your reason to expose your blindness, to strike your deadness, and to drive away your carelessness.

When so many subjects arise about which one must reason with himself, then it should not be supposed that only learned persons are able to accomplish this. Anyone can reason with himself about salvation, even a child. This is not the same as scientific reasoning. Every truth which is taken into the mind immediately and by itself inspires a person with that which it requires. Just be conscientious and restore within yourself a genuine desire

1   Isaiah 1:6
2   Cf. 2 Timothy 1:13
3   In Orthodoxy, each person who is serious about the spiritual life is encouraged to find a spiritual father, a priest or layperson experienced in the spiritual life who can guide the soul through the difficulties of this life so that the person can enjoy the fullness of the Christian life.

for good, with a willingness to follow the instructions of the truth.[4]

USE REASON TO AWAKEN YOUR SOUL

In every way possible, you must aim your reasoning towards the goal of acting on your soul in order to awaken and mobilize it to work for salvation. For this:

1 When you are considering a matter, do not philosophize, making up all sorts of questions for yourself. But having understood the subject of your reasoning, put the part that moves you the most into your heart and meditate upon it.[5]

2 Do not skip quickly from one idea to another. This will distract your thoughts rather than collecting them so that they can have an effect on the soul. The sun, for example, would not warm any creature on the earth if it moved over the face of the earth too quickly. Let the sympathy[6] of your heart to an idea be the full measure of your reasoning about this or that subject. Lead every idea to your deepest feelings and sensibilities, and do not retreat from it until it penetrates your heart.

3 If possible, do not leave an idea naked, in a rational form only. Clothe it in some kind of image and then carry it in your mind as a constant stimulus. Best of all—if it is possible—concentrate and focus in one image several striking presenta-

---

4   *Theophan's footnote:* Moreover, it is very useful to have ready to hand those edifying writings where the subjects about which one ought to reason with himself are revealed clearly and with authority. In this respect the writings of St. Tikhon of Zadonsk have an inestimable value, especially the articles about sin, about blindness, about the remission of sins to one who does not repent, and his private letters. For help in this very process of reasoning with oneself, look for the collected articles of the writings of the Church Fathers under the title, *Awake, O Sleeper.*

5   Literally, turn it to your heart with the side that you hope will make the strongest impression upon it, and then view it from that angle.

6   In Russian, the word *sympathy* has a different intensity than its English equivalent, and refers to the deepest kind of understanding. You might intellectually understand an idea, but you must bring it into the deepest sympathy of the heart to comprehend its essence fully. Sympathy is when the heart and mind come into full accord with each other. To do this typically requires a certain amount of time.

tions. St. Tikhon of Zadonsk writes in this vein, so that a sinner might impress upon his mind the danger of his situation. "Above you is the sword of truth, under you is hell which is ready to devour you, in front of you is death, behind you is the great multitude of your sins, on your right hand and on your left are crowds of malicious enemies. Do you wish to stay in carelessness?" An image is easier to remember and keep in mind, and it acts more powerfully, making a more vivid impression.

4   Select short but powerful sayings in conformity with your inner state, and then frequently repeat them to yourself, either mentally or vocally. For example:

- *The ox knows its owner, and the ass its master's manger,*[7] but you?
- Do you despise the riches and abundance of goodness, and the forbearance and patience of God?[8]
- Because of your stubbornness and unrepentant heart you are storing up wrath for yourself on the day of wrath and revelation of the righteous judgment of God.[9]
- *Watch therefore, for you do not know on what day your Lord is coming.*[10]
- Behold, the grave lies before me, behold death stands before me.[11]
- *Whither shall I go from thy Spirit? Or whither shall I flee from thy presence?*[12]
- *The wages of sin is death.*[13]
- *Be sober, be watchful. Your adversary the devil prowls around like a roaring lion, seeking someone to devour.*[14]
- Give an account of your management of the household.[15]
- *Everyone to whom much is given, of him will much be required.*[16]

7   Isaiah 1:3
8   Cf. Romans 2:4
9   Cf. Romans 2:5
10   Matthew 24:42
11   Taken from the evening prayers of the Orthodox prayer book.
12   Psalm 139:7
13   Romans 6:23
14   1 Peter 5:8
15   Cf. Luke 16:2
16   Luke 12:48

- *That servant who knew his master's will, but did not make ready or act according to his will, shall receive a severe beating.*[17]
- *Remember from what you have fallen, repent and do the works you did at first.*[18]

And so on . . .

Collect, memorize, and keep in mind such sayings as these and beat them into your heart. Perhaps one of them will become a fiery arrow which will strike you and kindle your heart into flame.

ALTERNATE REASON WITH PRAYER

Do not remain with reasoning alone, however, but alternate it with prayer. Now you must know that here we do the same as when we want to uproot a tree which has grown deep into the earth. We come to a tree and begin to shake it; exerting the strength of reasoning with ourselves, we urge and persuade ourselves. We shake it, but are not able to uproot it, because its roots have grown deep into the earth. We cannot uproot it because there is no strength within us of our own; consequently we have no power to cut off these roots. So, seek for help!

1 If, during your reflection, a certain feeling sinks into your heart, or if at any other time a certain deep warmth and tenderness awaken by themselves, then arise and pray.[19] Pray, so that God may sanctify your work with your stony petrified heart;[20] so that He may give this reflection the strength which both

---

17 Luke 12:47
18 Revelation 2:5
19 A deep feeling is likely to arise because of our reasoning, but it may arise at a time that is apart from our reasoning about spiritual matters. In both cases, the distinctive features of the feeling are the same: spiritual warmth, tenderheartedness, repentance, and so on. And in both cases, one should immediately arise and pray, to further develop this sympathy to the truth of God.

You should, however, note that not every sweetness that one feels in the heart is a sign of spiritual awakening. Rather, sometimes these sweet feelings are sentiment, which is quite divorced from the rigor of the true spiritual life. At other times these feelings may just be illusions created by our own desire. It is important to distinguish between them.

20 Ezekiel 11:19

destroys and creates; or so that He may, by Himself, come and soften, awaken, and wound.[21]

2   In this prayer, pray by yourself; speak about that which lies heavy upon your heart, and reveal your urgent needs in all confidence, with plain, childlike, and short words. But even better, fall down before God without words, in a painful appeal to Him.

3   Do not philosophize; do not compose your prayers. Draw near in simplicity with your need only—as a sick one draws near a doctor, as a prisoner to his deliverer, as a paralytic to the Lord—with a sincere and candid confession of your illness and your weak inability to overcome yourself, and entrust yourself to God's all-powerful action.

4   Fall prone before God; pray with prostrations and bows—many, many—and beat your breast.[22] Do not leave your prayer as long as it moves within you. When the prayer grows cold, then begin to reason and reflect again; and from this, move back to prayer.

5   For prayer as well as for reflection, select brief appeals to God and repeat them often:

• Have mercy on Your creature, O Master!

• *God, be merciful to me a sinner!*[23]

• Save now, I beseech thee, O Lord! O Lord, I beseech thee, send now succor![24]

     Remember the chants of the Orthodox Church that awaken and enliven you and chant them.

• "Behold, the Bridegroom comes in the middle of the night; and blessed is the servant whom He shall find watching, but unworthy is he whom He shall find in slothfulness. Beware,

---

21   Note the construction of this sentence: in the first case, you pray so that God blesses you as you work on your heart by yourself; in the second case, you pray so that He will strengthen you as you work; or in the third, you pray and He comes and works by Himself in your heart.

22   Cf. Luke 18:13

23   Luke 18:13

24   Cf. Psalm 118:25

then, O my soul, and be not overcome by sleep, lest thou be given over to death and shut out from the Kingdom. But return to soberness and cry aloud: Holy, holy, holy art Thou, O God: through the Theotokos have mercy upon us."[25]

- "As I ponder in my wretchedness the many evil things that I have done, I tremble for the fearful day of judgment. But trusting in Thy merciful compassion, like David do I cry to Thee: Have mercy upon me, O God, in Thy great mercy."[26]

- "My soul, O my soul, rise up! Why art thou sleeping? The end draws near, and so thou shalt be troubled. Watch, then, that Christ thy God may spare thee, for He is everywhere present and fills all things."[27]

Working hard on yourself in this way, knock incessantly at the door of God's mercy.[28]

SEEK GOD'S GRACE

What are we seeking through this work? We are seeking the activating grace of God. To influence us, God's grace is in the habit of choosing certain indirect means, as it was described above in the section on the extraordinary actions of God's grace. So, apply yourself to these indirect means and move under their influence. Will they not fall upon you as well, these rays of grace, as they have fallen upon other sinners like you?

1 God's grace has chosen for its action the churches of God and the divine services. So you too go to church and patiently, attentively, and reverently attend the celebration of divine services. The appearance of the church—together with its interior structure and decoration, the ritual structure of the divine

---

25 The Troparion of Holy and Great Wednesday. *The Lenten Triodion* (Mother Mary and Kallistos Ware, trans.). Boston: Faber and Faber, p. 535.

26 Chant from Sunday Matins. *The Lenten Triodion*, p. 101.

27 Kontakion of Thursday of the Great Canon, Matins. *The Lenten Triodion*, p. 399.

28 Matthew 7:7, 8

services, and the chanting with the readings—all these can act to produce their effect on you. So it is no wonder that, having entered into church empty and frivolous, you will leave it with the spirit of salvation.

2   Grace has acted through the Word of God. So you too take and read God's Word. Perhaps you will come across a passage which will strike you, as St. Augustine was struck when he opened the New Testament at random and his eyes fell upon a passage.[29]

3   The hearts of some sinners have been softened as a result of conversations with devout people. So you too go and have a talk with them. One word will lead to another in your conversation—and will there not fall such a word for you too, that will *pierce to the division of soul and spirit, discerning the thoughts and intentions of the heart?*[30] Perhaps the living Word, which is warmed by love, will pierce to the depth of your heart and shake the strongholds of sin that have formed there.

4   The prayers of the poor have been shown to be powerful and strong. So you too go and increase your almsgiving and charity. Dry the tears of the miserable. Settle, if you can, the lives of those who are ruined. The outcry of supplication from the poor reaches heaven and penetrates into the heaven of heavens. Will this outcry not also send you a guiding angel, as it did for Cornelius the centurion?[31]

Walking in the midst of these and similar exercises, you will touch the vessels and bearers of grace. Perhaps upon you too, from somewhere or other, its life-giving dew will descend and revive the sprouts of the spiritual life which have become frozen within you.

---

29   The passage which Augustine saw, in deep anguish about his sins of the flesh, was Romans 13:14: "Put on the Lord Jesus Christ, and make no provision for the flesh." Augustine did so, and in that moment was truly converted after many years of struggle.

30   Hebrews 4:12

31   Cf. Acts 10:1–8

9

The Importance of Ascetic Labors

When the intention to reform your life and your inward disposition comes, having driven away procrastination, restrain and lighten your flesh with bodily labors.[1] Put aside your everyday cares and distractions by stopping your ordinary activities for a time by means of solitude. Then, having concentrated your attention within yourself, strive hard to dispel your blindness, deadness, and carelessness by means of different saving thoughts, by reasoning with yourself and speaking with your soul. Alternate this with prayer, and put yourself under the influence of such circumstances as divine grace has already chosen as an indirect means for its action upon the souls of sinners.

Work, exert yourself. Seek, and you will find; knock, and it will be opened to you.[2] Do not relax and do not despair. But with all this, remember that your labors are only endeavors on your part for attracting grace. They are not the thing itself for which we are seeking. The principal thing that is lacking is the grace-given awakening and activation. This is very noticeable, whether we are reasoning or praying or doing something else. It is as if we are squeezing something alien into our hearts from the outside. According to the strength of our exertions in these labors, a particular effect will descend to a certain depth in the heart.

But afterwards it is again thrown out by a certain resistance of the recalcitrant, unruly, and unaccustomed heart, just as a stick that is vertically submerged in water is thrown out. Immediately after this displacement, coldness, estrangement, and coarseness again spring up in the heart. This is an obvious sign that there was

---

1   The Russian word here is *podvig*, which refers to bodily labors that are undertaken to facilitate an inward repentance.
2   Cf. Matthew 7:7, 8

no grace-given action or influence here, but only our work alone and our effort. Therefore, do not rest on these labors only, as though they were the very thing that you must acquire. This is a dangerous delusion![3] It is equally dangerous to think that there is merit in these labors, for which grace must necessarily be sent down. Not at all! This is only a preparation for its reception. The gift itself depends entirely upon the will of the Giver. So, making assiduous use of all the above-mentioned methods, the seeker should go on, expecting God's visitation, which does not come with observable signs—but when it comes, no one will know from whence it comes.[4]

Only after this awakening and activating grace comes will the real matter of reforming one's life and inward disposition begin. Without this one cannot expect a success; there will be only unsuccessful attempts. The witness to this is Blessed Augustine, who for a long time wore himself out by working on himself. He overcame himself only after grace blessed him. Work, then, expecting with sure trust the coming of God's grace. When grace comes, it will reestablish and restore all things.

---

3   In fact, this is *prelest,* the very dangerous sin of focusing on your own labors rather than on God. It is a kind of spiritual pride whereby the soul closes itself and separates from God, usually while thinking that it is drawing closer to God.
4   Cf. John 3:8

10

The Grace-Filled Awakening

It is natural to ask: What is the grace-filled awakening? In what state does it put a sinner? And how does this state differ from other, similar states? You must know the distinguishing features of this awakening, so that you do not pass over them fruitlessly and so that you do not mistake them for some natural state.

The state of the soul which is awakened and inspired by grace is defined in contrast with the state of the soul which has been put to sleep by sin.

1 Sin separates a man from God. A man, having deviated from God into sin, does not perceive or feel his dependence on Him. He lives as if he were not of God and God were not of him, like a willful servant who has run away from his master. Now the wall that has separated him is breaking down. *The perception and feeling of dependence on God* is being restored. A man is keenly aware of his entire subordination to God and his complete accountability before Him. Previously, heaven for him was made of copper and brass. It was as if there were a dense cover extending over his head. But now a certain beam of light passes through this dark and somber cover and points him toward God, who is both Master and at the same time, Judge. The perception and feeling of the Deity, together with all His perfections, is awakened and activated in him with power and stands unconquerably in the soul, filling it completely. Here is the foundation and the possibility for the future grace-filled spiritual life.

2 Previously sin had enveloped a man with blindness, deadness, and carelessness.[1] In the moment when grace strikes him, this

---

1   Theophan uses this formulation regularly throughout this text. These are the three main results that come from Satan's afflicting the soul.

three-layered petrified scale falls from the soul that has been imprisoned by it. Now a man *sees clearly all the ugliness and deformity within himself,* and not only sees, *but feels it as well.* At the same time he realizes the danger of his state, he begins to be afraid for himself and *to look after* his fate. And not only fearfulness sinks into the soul, but also—in the presence of the feeling of his accountability before God—dread, yearning, vexation, and shame begin to strike his heart powerfully and keenly. *Remorse of conscience gnaws* at him.

3   But at the same time, there is given to him a certain sensation of the sweetness of the life which is in accordance with the will of God. Now feeling all the obscenity and disgrace of the sinful life and having a loathing for it as for a sea of evil, he also has an anticipation that comfort and solace are concealed in this domain of good, which now has opened to the eye of his soul. This domain is viewed as the Promised Land, as a place which is the most blessed and safest from all the great agitations and troubles. This very anticipation is a manifestation in the sinful soul, which a man cannot produce by any means of his own. These are blessings and gifts of God and are under His power and authority. To think about them does not mean one feels them. God introduces the spirit of a man to His treasure-house and gives the spirit a taste of its blessings.

4   Note how necessary this action of God's mercy and kindness is on the way leading to the liberation of the soul from the power and authority of sin. The goal and strength of the grace-given awakening and activation is in the fact that it extricates a man from the jaws of sin and places him on the balance point between good and evil. The scales of our will, in which it sometimes leans to one side and sometimes to the other, now must be on the same level. But there will be no balance if the sinner does not taste the sweetness of the good, at least through anticipation. If this were not given, then the sweetness of sin, as something which has already been experienced, would have attracted him to itself more powerfully than the

good; and the choice would always fall to the side of sin. This usually happens when someone intends to change his life without a grace-given awakening. For this the general rule is: *ignoti nulla cupido;* that is, what one does not know, he cannot desire. But, when he is given to taste the sweetness of the good in a grace-given awakening and inspiration, then it also begins to attract him to itself as something which has already been experienced, known, and felt. The scales are equal. Now complete freedom of action rests in the hands of a man.

5   So, in the presence of the grace-given awakening and inspiration—as with the brilliance of lightning—everything within a man and around him is illuminated. Now, for a moment, he is introduced by his heart into the order from which he was previously cast out by sin. He is inserted into the chain of creation, into that communion from which he had been willfully[2] thrown out by his sin. That is why this action of grace is almost always characterized by fear and by an instantaneous shock; as one who is hastily walking while lost in his thoughts is shocked by a sudden shout, "Stop!" If one looks at this state from the standpoint of psychological thought, then it is nothing less than the awakening of the spirit. As a matter of fact, it is natural for our spirit to know the Deity and a certain higher world or order of things. It is natural for our spirit to lift a man up over everything that is sensual and to carry him away into a purely spiritual domain. But in the sinful state our spirit loses its power and becomes mingled with the lower natural instincts, and through them with sensuality to such an extent that it, as it were, disappears beneath them. So now the spirit is extracted by grace and placed as it were on a lampstand within our inner dwelling-place, so that it can give light to everything that is there within us and to everything that can be made visible from there.

---

2   That is, the man chose by his own will to sin rather than to live in accordance with the will of God. So Theophan speaks of his "willfulness" in being thrown out of the communion that exists in the created order.

DIFFERENTIATING THIS AWARENESS
FROM NATURAL STATES

The state in which the soul is placed in the grace-given awakening is similar to many natural states, with which it must not be confused.

1   In the presence of the grace-given state, a man stands in a certain painful and sorrowful sense of dissatisfaction with himself and his situation. This, however, is different from *melancholy*. There is no definite object in melancholy: here a man sorrows and grieves, not knowing why or over what he grieves. In the grace-given awakening and inspiration, however, there is a definite object for one's grieving, namely, the insulting of God and the defiling of oneself. Melancholy is a property of our fallen nature, but this state is spiritual.[3] The former is tormenting, dismal, and killing. That is why it is said, "One is choked with grief." But the latter is life-giving and awakens and activates you to genuine life.

There are many such indefinite grievings in our ordinary life, and each one has its own shades. Among them, one is worthy of particular mention: the yearning for our heavenly homeland, the feeling of dissatisfaction with every created thing, and the sense of spiritual hunger. This also is one of the natural motions of the spirit. When, little by little, the passions are stilled, the spirit raises its outcry, which is distinctly echoed in the heart. It lifts up its voice about the straitened and humiliated condition in which it is held, and asks why it is not properly fed, but made to suffer hunger. This is the deep yearning for the spirit's homeland,[4] the groaning which the Apostle heard in the whole creation.[5] Nevertheless, this is not the same as the grace-given awakening and inspiration. It is one of the natural motions or functions of our spirit, which by itself is mute and without fruit. The grace-given awakening

3   Cf. 2 Corinthians 7:10
4   Cf. Hebrews 11:13–16
5   Cf. Romans 8:22, 23

and inspiration descends upon it and imparts to it a brightness and liveliness.

2   In the presence of the grace-given awakening and inspiration, there is *contrition* and the *breaking of the spirit,*[6] the awakening of a *disturbed conscience.*[7] However, this is absolutely not the same as ordinary annoyance with ourselves for slips in our daily life, even those which are more or less substantial. We torment ourselves when we say something improper, when we do something improper, and in general, in all those occurrences where we have brought shame upon ourselves. We even say, "Oh, shame on me!" But this is not the voice of the spirit's conscience that is now heard.

There a man has in mind only himself and his transient and ephemeral relationships; but here, on the contrary, he completely forgets himself and everything that is transient and ephemeral, and sees only God alone, whom he has insulted, and his broken relationship with the Eternal. There he stands for himself and for the rules and principles of men, but here he stands for God's will and His glory. There he grieves that he has brought shame upon himself before others, but here he grieves that he has brought shame upon himself before God; and he does not care what people say or even for the opinion of the whole world. Besides, there the grief is inconsolable, while here it is somewhat mitigated by a certain solace and consolation. For there all his support is upon himself and others, and when this foundation has been destroyed, he has nowhere to turn. But here everything is from God, by whom he does not expect to be rejected, but in whom he trusts and hopes.

Our ordinary consciousness of our mistakes imitates the actions of true conscience.[8] One may say that they are also

6   Cf. Psalm 51:17; Isaiah 57:15; 66:2
7   This *disturbed conscience* is understood as a positive occurrence. Disturbances of this nature cause a person to think about his condition and move him to action.
8   Both *consciousness* and *conscience* stem from the same Latin root, meaning "to have knowledge of, to be aware of." This parallel is identical with the Russian usage.

actions of the conscience, but a conscience which is distorted and degraded from its true standing. Together with the spirit it also has fallen from its natural height and from the spiritual domain, and has fallen into the hands and under the dominion of the lower animal nature. It has begun to serve worldly aims only. It has become, so to speak, a worldly and profane conscience, which more strongly feels insults towards men than towards God.

3   In the presence of the grace-given awakening and inspiration, it is given to the heart to perceive a different kind of life, which is much better, much more perfect, and joyous. This, however, is absolutely not the same as what happens to those who feel an awakening of those bright aspirations and noble impulses, which might be better called "an agitation of ideas." These phenomena are similar in that they both lift a man up over his usual routine and steer him towards the realization of these ideas; but they diverge vastly in their directions, destinations, and goals. The latter directs a man into an uncertain and hazy domain; but the former leads to God, points to a peaceful rest in Him, and gives a foretaste of that peace. The goal of the former is life in God together with everlasting bliss. The latter always intends something great and special, of course, but it always remains vague—a "something."

But the most striking difference is in the fact that these bright aspirations and noble impulses show up and act erratically: here the spirit inspires one man from one side and another man from another side. The grace-given awakening, however, embraces the entire spirit from all sides, and places it by its goal, satisfies it, or grants it a foretaste of the full and complete satisfaction of this divine order. The impulses of the highest aspirations of the spirit are the remnants of God's image in a man[9]—of the image that is broken. That is why they manifest themselves in a way similar to splintered and dispersed

9   Cf. Genesis 1:27

beams of light. One must gather these beams together into one to concentrate them, and then a burning ray will be formed. The grace that awakens the spirit produces this very concentration of the beams of the spirit—which is one in itself, but which has been splintered in the many-sided soul. In this way grace kindles the fire for the spiritual life, placing a man not in a cold contemplation, but in a certain life-giving and burning ardor.

Such a gathering of the spirit into one focuses the feeling on the Deity: here is embryonic life. So it is in nature as well. Life does not come into being as long as its powers act separately; but as soon as the Most High has gathered them together into one, then immediately a living creature comes into existence—a plant, for example. So it is also in the spirit: as long as its inclinations manifest themselves separately, now one and now another, one in this direction and the other in that, there is no life within him. But when the most high divine power of grace, providentially steering the spirit, gathers together all its aspirations into one and holds them in this single beam, then the burning ardor of the spiritual life arises within a man.

By these signs you can easily distinguish the grace-given awakening and inspiration from the ordinary phenomena of the spiritual life within a man, so that you might not confuse them, and above all, so that you might not let slip the opportunity to avail yourself of this awakening and inspiration for your salvation. This must be known especially by those upon whom God's grace acts without their own preliminary labors, and by those upon whom it acts without any special intensity. It is impossible to ignore this state of awakening and inspiration, but it is possible not to give it enough attention and, upon having dwelt in it a little, to descend once again into the usual routine of the movements of the soul and body. This awakening and inspiration does not complete the matter of the conversion of a sinner, but merely begins it. After the awakening comes, the work of self-perfection lies ahead—work that is very complicated. Everything, however, that is related to this work is accomplished in two turnings, both made by one's free will: the first movement of a sinner is towards self, and the second is from self to God. In the first turning a man regains his lost mastery over himself, and in the second, he offers himself as a sacrifice to God[10]—the burnt offering of his freedom. In the first, he reaches the point at which he decides to renounce sin, and in the second, drawing near to God, he makes the vow to belong to Him alone all the days of his life.

10   Cf. Romans 12:1

11

The Ascent of a Sinner

Whether grace visits someone by itself, or whether someone seeks for it and finds it—the state in which it places a man during its first action upon him is identical in both cases. An awakened and activated one is placed by grace in a neutral state between sin and virtue. Grace extracts him from the bonds of sin, having deprived sin of its power and authority to determine his actions against his will. But grace does not move him over to the side of goodness. It merely allows him to feel its superiority, consolation, and joy together with the feeling of commitment to be on the side of the good. Now that a man stands at the crossroads, a decisive choice lies ahead of him.

St. Macarius of Egypt says (his first word on keeping a watchful guard over the heart, Chapter 12) that the grace which comes to a man does not in the least "bind his free will by a forcible power and does not establish him immutably in the good, even if he desired this or did not desire it. On the contrary, even God's power, which is inherent in a man, gives a place to freedom in order that the will of a man might manifest itself—whether it conforms to grace or not." From this minute on, the conjoining of man's freedom with God's grace begins.

Previously grace acted upon a man from without, and stood outside of him. Now grace enters within and begins to lay hold of parts of the spirit. This occurs when a man, by his free will, opens the door in himself, or when he opens his lips for receiving it. When a man desires and wills grace, it is ready with assistance. By himself, a man cannot make or confirm the good within himself, but wills it and strains himself towards it. For the sake of this willing, grace strengthens the good within a man, the good which he desires and wills. Everything will go precisely in this way until a man finally takes possession of himself with respect to doing good and pleasing God.

DECIDING TO LEAVE SIN

Everything that a man must do in this work of self-perfection and the manner in which he reaches the decision to leave sin is the same as when we make up our mind to do any other kind of matter. Usually, after the thought of doing something comes into our mind, we incline to this thought with our will; we remove any obstacles and make up our mind to do it. Precisely the same thing happens in deciding to live the Christian life. One must:

1 by one's will, incline oneself towards the Christian life;
2 remove any inner obstacles which would interfere with making a decision; and
3 decide.

Although the action of grace places the spirit in an awakened and activated state, nevertheless its suggestion to reform one's life is merely a thought. This thought, however, is more or less active and lively: "Maybe I should leave sin," or "I must leave sin." One who is awakened from a dream sees that it is time and he must get up. But in order to get up, he must make some particular exertions; he must make particular movements with different parts of the body. He stretches his muscles, throws off his covers, and gets up.

So, having felt the grace-filled awakening and inspiration within yourself, hurry to incline your will to its demands, consent to its suggestion that it is necessary for you—you who cannot justify yourself before God and who are impure—to reform yourself, and to set about this *immediately.*

For one who sought for grace-given help and who now feels its visitation, such a willing must be present. It has already guided you in all the above-mentioned labors; but here to its composition and for its accomplishment something else is added. There is a mental willing: the intellect demands and a man forces himself. Such a willing governs the preparatory labors. There is a sympathetic willing: it arises under the action of the grace-given awakening and inspiration. Finally, there is an active willing: the consent of the will to set to the work of rising from your falls and transgressions immediately. Now, after the awakening of the spirit, active willing must be formed. This is the first work of the inspired one after his awakening.

That not everyone who is awakened sets to the work of reforming his life for the better is known to all. So also, not everyone who awakens from sleep gets up from his bed immediately, but it happens that several times he falls asleep again.

On the one hand, the grace-given awakening places a man in an advantageous and active state; but on the other hand, it sets up demands which are rather constraining. One who will now rely more on the first side may permit himself "the soaring of thoughts" and prematurely indulge in the joy of life, as if he had everything that he should have. But this indulgence will not allow one to pay proper attention to what has happened, and the inward distraction which is joined to this indulgence will soon make one cool—and the opportune moment and the favorable inward state will be missed. Again the usual coarseness and hardness comes, in the presence of which one cannot master oneself.

On the other hand, the one who relies more upon the side of constraining demands may permit himself a little release from this constraint, as a child who throws off a bandage with curative plaster merely because it constricts him. In this situation, a person—in order to dispel his gloomy thoughts—sets about ostensibly innocent diversions: conversations or reading. Another person may begin to scrutinize the painful feeling which has arisen within him, in order to try to find out why and how it could form. In the first case with the diversions, there are foreign and extraneous impressions, but in the second case, there is the disintegrating action of scrutinizing—both of which erase the saving changes taking place within a sinner. In the end, both fall into their habitual immovable coarseness and hardness.

It seems that this should not happen. This takes place,

however, because the grace-given inspirations have different degrees, and the circumstances in which they come can be such as to obscure the significance and value of their appearance within a sinner. God's all-wise grace permits this, testing the free will of a man. That is why we say, as soon as you have sensed within yourself the grace of awakening and inspiration and you realize what it is, then hurry to incline your will to its suggestions. And for this:

1   Believe in the simplicity of your heart that this is from God, that God Himself calls you to Himself and that He Himself draws near to you in order to bring forth the saving change within you.

2   Having believed, do not allow yourself to lose this action of God's lovingkindness without bearing fruit. This awakening and inspiration alone gives you the power to overcome yourself. If it is withdrawn, you will not by yourself be able to overcome yourself. And whether it will come again, this you cannot say. Perhaps for the last time this condescension comes to you. Afterwards, you will fall into hardness of heart, and from this, into despondency and hopelessness.

3   As much as you can, exert every effort and use your best endeavors to keep yourself in that saving state in which you have been placed. Just as a flammable substance that is placed before a fire not only gets warm but can catch fire, so naturally desire for the grace-given life can be kindled if one keeps oneself under the influence of grace for as long as possible.

4   So push aside everything that can extinguish this little fire which is being kindled in you and surround yourself with everything that can feed it and bring it to a blaze. Seclude yourself;[1] pray and reflect with yourself how you should be. That order of life—those activities and labors which were pointed out and which you have forced yourself to pursue in seeking

---

1   This call to seclude oneself is not meant to imply that everyone should retire to a monastery like Theophan. Rather, it means that everyone who is serious about the spiritual life should find opportunities to go into solitude—even in the midst of everyday life—perhaps just one or two hours a day.

for grace—is also the most favorable for prolonging the action of grace which has begun within you. And the best of these activities are solitude,[2] prayer, and careful reflection.[3] Reason with yourself. Think through all the ideas which you gathered previously while trying to drive away your blindness, deadness, and carelessness. Even if these three are not present now, you still must kindle the desire to begin the work immediately. Direct all your efforts to precisely this. Now, your reasoning with yourself will not be the same as it was before. Without awakening and inspiration, your reasoning usually deviates by reflecting about spiritual subjects in general, without reference to yourself. Now, on the contrary, following the lead of grace and under its guidance, your reasoning will refer everything exactly to you yourself. Without any excuses or deviations, it will direct your reflection to you yourself, utilizing those aspects which will have the most effect on you.[4] That

---

2   In the Orthodox tradition, solitude is not a passive activity, a going apart to be passively receptive to God. Rather, it is an active state wherein the person is fully engaged in the praxis of moving into God. This view is considerably different from similar ideas of the Western Church, which variously see solitude as an opportunity to cultivate a passive receptivity to God, or as an escape into quietism.

3   This word, which we have often translated as "reasoning," carries the notion of reflection: the fixing of the mind on some spiritual subject, and pondering that subject thoroughly. In current Western usage, we do not think of reasoning as a spiritual exercise. But for the Church Fathers and with St. Theophan as a continuer of the patristic tradition, reasoning has an important place in spiritual development.

4   There are many medications which may have a salutary effect upon people. But if you do not know that you are ill, you have only a cursory interest in them. Once you know that you are ill, however, you take a very personal interest in these different medicines. You go to the doctor by your free will, and he prescribes specific medications which will have the most effect upon you. And then you use them regularly until your full recovery, even if they are not pleasant to take.

In a like manner, when you are spiritually unwell you turn to the Heavenly Physician asking for assistance, and you become very interested in the specific medications which apply to your soul's health. At the beginning of the spiritual journey, the best medications for the sinful soul are solitude, prayer, and reasoning. God directs your reasoning to those medicines that will have the most effect upon you. Before, you may not have been interested in them, or you thought about them only in a general way. Now, however, you apply them to yourself with great interest, for the specific purpose of restoring your spiritual health.

is why, strictly speaking, you will not so much reason as pass from feeling to feeling.

"I WILL BEGIN"

Finally, in this work of perfecting yourself with the help of grace, there will be uttered in your heart a word which can only be heard by you and God: "It is necessary, so I will begin immediately." Apparently, this is the conclusion; but according to what laws and from what statutes it is derived, no science can determine. All the subjects of previous reasonings can be known clearly, but this conclusion cannot be. It even happens that one person may strongly set forth all these matters in words, and tens and hundreds reach this conclusion from the action of his words, but in his own heart it is not uttered. And nobody can say who[5] is acting here—grace or free will. For it happens that sometimes the grace-filled action passes by in vain, and all the efforts and exertions of your free will remain fruitless. Both are combined in a way that is incomprehensible and unfathomable to us; yet each one preserves its own nature. You might say free will entrusts itself to grace, and grace accepts and permeates it. From here the power of desire arises: "So, immediately set to work!"

Here at last, a man is leaning in the direction of goodness. He is willing to enter this holy way; he is willing to walk in good deeds by pleasing God. But in this moment, the entire abyss of evil which was hiding in his heart is swept up like dust and strives to cover the entire soul again. In the moment of awakening and inclining towards the good, sin is silent, as if what takes place within a man does not matter to it. But now, when one wants to trample sin underfoot, the thousand-headed monster, as St. John Climacus in his *Ladder of Divine Ascent* calls it, utters a thousand curses upon the man who proposes doing this.

5   The use of *who* in this context is unusual in Russian as well as English. Theophan, by using *who*, emphasizes that persons are acting here—God or human beings—rather than the attributes of these persons, such as grace and free will.

This is similar to a person who is awake, and is just thinking of getting up—everything in his body is quiet and calm. But as soon as he proposes to get up in actual fact and exert his muscles a little, all the aches in his body, which did not disturb him previously, now reveal themselves and make their complaint. So also with one who inclines toward the grace-given call. The sinful pains are silent until he comes to this inclination; but as soon as he proposes to set about this work, all these infirmities raise a strong and troubling alarm. Thoughts and emotions race through him, one after another, striking the poor man and pulling him backwards. Attacking without any order from all sides, they envelop the soul and submerge it in their agitation. Every good thing within a man hangs as if by a thread, and he himself is ready to break contact at any moment with that by which he is supported, and so submerge himself again in the same conditions from which he had previously been willing to leave. One thing saves him—the taste of that sweetness, favor, comfort, and joy which were bestowed on him in the moment of awakening, and that strength which he felt when he uttered: "So, I will immediately begin."

One who has seen how a little spark darts here and there in the smoke, trying to preserve its life; or how a small twig is thrown by a turbulent stream, now upwards, now downwards, at another moment to the right and then to the left—he has in these images what happens to the good intentions of a man in this moment. Not only is there confusion and agitation in the soul, but also his blood boils, and sometimes there is even a buzzing in his ears and a mist before his eyes. It is not difficult to understand that such a rebellion is not just from the sin which is dwelling in his heart, but from the father of all sins—the devil, who cannot remain at rest when such an agitator appears in his kingdom.

St. Tikhon of Zadonsk says, "When a sinner, who has pushed forward by the help of God's grace, begins to repent, then he encounters various diverse temptations. When a man begins to draw near to Christ, then Satan follows him and distracts him from Christ; he spreads his nets and trips him up."

There is a story about terrifying and seductive ghosts that are encountered by those who go looking for buried treasure. This psychological myth best describes the actions of the devil, who tries his best to distract a man from his good intention *to buy the pearl of great price* [6] or *to find the treasure hidden in the field.* [7]

It is precisely here that a hard struggle with himself is in store for a man, a decisive battle with sin. Here he must resolutely capture and defeat his enemy, tread upon this serpent, [8] bind him, and exhaust his every power. The successful conquering of sin here is the basis for the hope and efficacy of all subsequent masterings of sin in their particular insurrections. It is not possible to define everything that takes place here, due to the variety and diversity of people and occasions for sin. However, the principal points—the turning points of this struggle—are not difficult to indicate. We mark them for the assistance of those who are struggling against sin rather than for the sake of intellectual acquisition.

Apparently there is no point of support in the soul: it vacillates, though it is still whole and not yet broken in its good intention, being succored by God's grace. But who else will support it; who will establish it firmly? That is why what now lies ahead for a soul above all else is the persistent calling upon God, like the cries of one who is drowning. The enemy has grabbed you and wants to swallow you up—cry to the Lord like Jonah in the fish's belly, [9] or like the drowning Peter. [10] The Lord sees your need and your labor, and He will stretch forth His hand and take hold of you and establish you as a warrior who is setting out for combat.

Here there is support! The most dangerous thing is for the soul to try to find support within itself; then it will lose everything. Evil will again overcome the soul; it will darken this light in the soul, which for the time being is faint. It will extinguish this

6   Matthew 13:45, 46
7   Matthew 13:44
8   Cf. Genesis 3:15
9   Cf. Jonah 2:2, 3
10 Cf. Matthew 14:28–33

little fire which has just barely been kindled. The soul knows how weak and infirm it is by itself; that is why, expecting nothing from itself, the soul must fall down in shame before God. Let the soul in its heart reduce itself to *nothing*. Then, from this *nothing*, the almighty grace of God will create everything in it. One who puts himself in the hand of God—by means of the most extreme self-humiliation[11]—attracts Him who is tenderhearted, and he will be made powerful by His power.

In the presence of all this self-humiliation, however, you must not fall into an exhaustion of the soul. Having committed yourself to God, you must not give yourself over to inactivity. No, expecting everything from God and nothing from yourself, you must exert yourself to action, and act according to your strength so that there will be something to which divine assistance might come, and in order that there might be something for the divine power to protect. Grace is already present, but it will act immediately after your own actions, filling up your powerlessness by its power. So, having established yourself firmly in self-humiliation and prayerful submission to the will of God, work without slackening.

WORK AGAINST THE INCITERS OF SIN

Work against sin in general, but especially against its fundamental inciters. When everything in the soul is agitated, and thoughts envelop it like phantoms, directing their arrows from all sides right to the heart—it is not difficult to notice the main inciters of evil. Behind the multitude of auxiliary soldiers, the main warriors stand there at the very back: those who give the orders and instructions

---

11 The notion of self-humiliation is foreign and even repugnant to a culture rooted in concepts like self-esteem, positive regard, and the like. Theophan means that we acknowledge the shame that comes from understanding that we have deliberately turned away from our true nature, created in the image of God, in order to embrace and be something less. Understood in this way, Theophan is simply exhorting us, in the words of a contemporary recruiting slogan, to "Be all that you can be!"

and who manage the course of the battle. These are precisely the fundamental inciters of sin. You must direct all your attention precisely to them, arm yourself straight against them, subdue and annihilate them. When they are overcome,[12] the auxiliary soldiers will disperse by themselves.

What are these main inciters of sin and the principal warriors that defend it? This was pointed out by the Savior when He invited the people to come after Him (Mark 8:34–38). He said, "If any man would come after Me, *let him deny himself.*" Let him turn away from himself, consider himself as though alien to himself, as one who does not deserve attention or sympathy, as one for whom it is not even worthwhile to stand. This presupposes that in the sin-loving heart there is permanently present a disposition opposed to this—which is in fact *self-pity*. A man-sinner[13] treats himself as a loving mother treats her tenderly loved child: he cannot bear to deny himself or thwart himself in anything; he cannot overcome himself or punish himself. However, the Savior obliges a man to deny himself everything that is in the world[14] for the sake of his salvation. *For what does it profit a man, to gain the whole world and forfeit his soul?*[15] The world is the totality of things that are outside of us; that is, everything that is visible, tangible, and sensual. Consequently, the cited obligation presupposes that in the heart of a man there is a disposition towards material things, a greediness for the tangible, a certain passion to feed on and to indulge in the visible and sensual alone.

And in fact, *sensuality* is present in a lover of sin; he has no taste for the invisible and spiritual. Everything that is sensual is so familiar, and is often and deeply experienced. The Lord impresses upon us that we are not to be ashamed of Him and His words in this adulterous and sinful generation. This causes us to suppose[16]

---

12   Cf. Ephesians 6:10–18
13   *Man-sinner* is Theophan's construction, and is equally unusual in Russian as it is in English.
14   Cf. 1 John 2:15–17
15   Mark 8:36
16   Theophan is working backwards here. Taking Christ's words about not being

that in a sin-loving heart there is shame which works to the detriment of the good and the truth. This is precisely so. Usually a man lives by the inviolable routine, customs, and relations which have been established around him. That is why he is timid about challenging them. To support these customs, he is sometimes ready to go against his conscience rather than to act counter to someone, rather than not humor him, rather than cause trouble with him. This is *man-pleasing:*[17] "What would people say and how should I be, if I have to break off my connections?" This must be the most sensitive[18] of sin's bonds, since in order to break free from it, a man has to be threatened with the price of being shamed at the Universal Judgment: *For whoever is ashamed of Me and of My words in this adulterous and sinful generation, of him will the Son of man also be ashamed, when He comes in the glory of His Father with the holy angels.*[19]

This conclusion, directing us to the age to come, points out the lack of feeling for the future life in the sin-loving heart. It causes one to suppose that there is no other life for him, and so his heart is wholly submerged in the present life. This is precisely so. Usually a man lives on the earth as though he were going to live here forever, and he forgets about the future. He knows only worldly happiness, and all his goals converge on one thing: how shall he spend this life well. What will come later he does not even consider.

So, *self-pity, sensuality, man-pleasing,* and *earthliness* (i.e., the belief that there is no life beyond this earthly existence) are the distinctive characteristics of the sin-loving heart. Consequently, they are also the fundamental inciters of sin and the principal warriors in defense of it. We sinners would not be able to discover

ashamed of Him, he asks what might the Lord be referring to. Theophan concludes that there is a shame in us that works against the good.

17   This technical term is a single word in Russian. It is the opposite of *God-pleasing,* the process of conforming one's life to be in accord with God's will.

18   This is an odd usage. Contextually Theophan would seem to be saying that this is the most *resistant* of sin's bonds.

19   Mark 8:38

them by ourselves, and had the Savior not pointed them out to us, we would not even have been aware of them. But now that they have been disclosed, it is evident that this must be precisely so. A man fallen away from God has turned to himself and is punished by self-pity: this results from the principal property of the Fall. The fallen man has become disordered within himself; from the spirit, he fell into the flesh and languishes there in sensuality. The chief arena in which sin reveals itself and rages is the society of sinners, with such orders, customs, and mutual relationships between them as feed and support sin. When in these tollhouses of sin everything goes well, there is happiness and good fortune. But since such a course of life can only be in this age (for the future age requires an entirely different one), then not even a thought is given to the future age. It is not placed in one's mind, and all the more, it does not find sympathy in the heart.

Precisely in this way, these very roots of sin are the inciters of all thoughts which rise up against a man when he is willing to make a step from the domain of sin to the side of good. They raise up a whole swarm of tempting and captivating thoughts which confuse and terrify him, and suppress his good intentions.

Self-pity cries out, "What kind of life is this? Ahead are only labors, hardships, afflictions, and privations whose end cannot be seen. It is like walking among thorn bushes with thistles under your bare feet—there will be wounds every moment!"

Sensuality gives its vote: "You leave one thing and another, and you stop doing this thing and that—in a word, everything that I have found a taste for—and you occupy yourself with spiritual things alone! This is too abstract, dry, unhealthy, and lifeless!"

Man-pleasing complains, "What will people say? They will consider you strange and begin to avoid you; meanwhile you will have to break off this connection and another—but how will you be afterwards? And from other quarters, you can even expect enmity."

And there is the clamor of *earthliness:* "The future certainly will come to pass—who argues against that—but it is still a long way off. For now, how should you live your life? Others lived out their lives in this way, didn't they . . . The earthly life we know; but what will that other life be like? This life is in our hands, but where is that other?"

Yes, as soon as a man begins to serve the Lord, all these at once will cry out at him. If only these were some light or easy thoughts, but they are not. On the contrary, they pierce to the bottom of his soul. They strike a man, and draw him to their side just like someone hooking his own flesh with a fishing rod and pulling it to himself. What can be done for a man in this situation?

EXERT YOURSELF

Help is near . . . you only need to exert some effort and you will overcome, but make your efforts expediently. Having established yourself, as was said above, in prayer, in a self-humiliating trust in the will of God and in His all-powerful grace:

1   Hurry to drive all these thoughts out of your soul. Force them out of your consciousness by means of a special exertion of your own activity. Squeeze them back into that secret place from which they came and restore your peace of heart, because until the heart has become quiet, nothing further will be possible. From the very first, do not occupy yourself with these thoughts at all and do not enter into conversation with them, even an antagonistic conversation. A mob of rude illiterates soon scatters if you treat them sternly from the first; but if you speak a lenient word to one, to a second, and to a third, then they pluck up their courage and become more insistent in their demands. So also a mob of tempting and captivating thoughts becomes more demanding if you allow them to linger a little in the soul, and all the more if, in addition, you enter into negotiations with them. But if from the first you push them away with mighty exertions of the will, rejecting them and turning to God, then they will immediately withdraw, leaving the atmosphere of the soul clean and pure.

2   But even if this dark horde of wicked thoughts is driven away,

even if the heart again is quiet and the soul becomes pure and bright—you must remember that here, strictly speaking, your work is not finished. All these enemies are still alive. They are merely forced out of your attention. They have probably intentionally hidden themselves in order to attack unexpectedly at an opportune time, so much the more reliably to regain the victory for themselves. No, you should not stop here, otherwise you will have neither peace nor success. It is necessary to slay them. You must entice them out and slaughter them on the altar of self-denial.

TURNING THE HEART

So, having established yourself again in prayerful commitment to God and to His grace, summon each of these inciters of sin and strive to turn your heart away from them and to turn it towards the opposite. By this means, these inciters of sin will be cut off from the heart and will wither away. For this, give freedom to sound reasoning, and guide your heart along its tracks. Let your reasoning[20]—which has been brightened by the truth and which has been mysteriously assisted by active grace:

1   First, imagine all the deformity and ugliness of these offspring of hell. Force your heart to feel an *aversion and disgust* for them.

2   Then, clearly imagine the danger into which they throw you and let your reasoning point out the fiercest enemies. You, in your turn, compel your heart to conceive a *hatred* for them.

3   Then, more fully imagine all the beauty and sweetness of the life that they prevent you from entering, and all your delight in freedom from these tyrants. You, in your turn, strain your heart—which has already conceived an aversion and disgust for them—*to rush* from this enemy towards the spiritual world, as the deer pants for the water brooks.[21]

---

20   Reasoning seems here to be imaginative in nature: bringing to mind a certain image, then tracing the development of that image. This is not so much verbal reasoning as it is reflection or even meditation.
21   Cf. Psalm 42:1

By means of this, you will attain your goal. This program is short, but the work itself may not be accomplished so quickly. Here there have been pointed out only the subjects to which your reasoning must be directed; but everyone should carry out this line of reasoning by himself until it reaches its goal. In your own reasoning, the strength and efficacy of each idea is better seen in one respect or another. You must know, however, that this reasoning is only a lever; the substance of the work consists in turning the heart. One may say that as soon as the indicated changes have taken place in the heart, then we are near the goal.

This labor is the most essential part in the work of making a radical change of one's will. One should labor actively and energetically, and not step back until the heart reaches, in these turnings, its last limits. These last limits are *the feelings of antipathy* towards the sinful agitations—that inward disposition which is opposed to the fundamental demands and claims of sin. Thus, one must constantly labor at perfecting oneself until:

- instead of *self-pity*—*pitilessness* towards self and mercilessness revives, until a thirst for suffering begins to be felt, a desire to exhaust oneself, to weary one's body and soul;
- instead of *man-pleasing,* first a *disgust and turning away* from all evil customs and connections which have arisen—a certain irritation, a hostile resistance to them; and second—*a dooming of self* to all the injustices, falsehoods, and slander that come from people;
- instead of a *taste* for the material, sensual, and visible alone, there comes a *distaste and abhorrence* for it, and seeking and thirsting commence for the spiritual, the pure, and the divine;
- instead of *earthliness*—the restriction of life and happiness to this earth alone—the feeling that one is a *stranger and a pilgrim on this earth* [22] has filled one's heart with the sole yearning for the Heavenly Fatherland.

---

22 Cf. 1 Peter 2:11

EXPLODING THE SUPPORTS OF SIN

When such dispositions are formed, then all the supports of sin will be exploded. They will lose their steadfastness and directing power, which will now pass to the person himself. Sin is thrown out; it now stands outside. From this minute on it will no longer be determinative; it will only be tempting and seductive. And each time it tempts you, you need only put into motion those acquired feelings which are opposed to sin in order to drive it away. From this you can see the great importance of the labor which was described above. By means of it the new man is formed within us, with a resolute and decisive turning away from evil and a striving towards good. A radical change of will is being accomplished, and as a result, everything within us must assume a new order.

Here a man stands on the very edge of the sinful domain—nothing separates him from the land of light, freedom, and bliss. The fetters have fallen off, the soul is light and joyful; it is ready to soar up to God. But the craft and guile of the enemy are not yet exhausted. He has one more arrow which he has reserved for the last minute.

Just as the soul exerts its strength to make the last step out of the domain of self-indulgent sin, a piteous cry strikes its attention: "Just one more day and that will be enough—tomorrow you will step across the border." Whether the soul is tired from the previous struggle and needs a rest, or because sin has had such a command over it, the fact is that this voice is heard. The soul does not seem to oppose the good, but merely asks to loosen a little the tension which it has acquired. This cry is the most enticing: the enemy ostensibly stands up for us; he implores us to take pity on ourselves. But just yield a little to this cry, to this suggestion, and you will lose everything that you have acquired. By some secret mysterious paths, these banished inciters of sin will steal up to the heart and, without your knowledge, commit fornication with it. And everything that was conceived and intended they will enervate and put into disorder so that you, having come to yourself, see yourself in your previous state, as if you had done nothing to perfect yourself. Coldness, hardness, and sluggishness will again overcome you—it comes to the point where you have to begin all over again.

Therefore do not underestimate this, as though it were some insignificant request. It is small and insignificant in appearance, but in fact it is the sum of all evil, a charming but delusive representation of slavery under the guise of freedom. It is a flattering friendship which conceals the implacable and uncompromising enemy.

Feel a hatred for this with all your power,[23] and as soon as you observe it (it flies through quickly, like lightning) hurry to eradicate its trace so that not even the sign of it will remain. Place yourself in the same state that you were before, and resolve to hold yourself forever in the same inward and outward tension. Having struck down this enemy also, you will remain the resolute and decisive victor who has pulled himself together. You will be completely your own master.

Thus, right after the awakening and inspiration of grace, *the first thing* that lies ahead for the free will of a man is the *movement towards self,* which it accomplishes in three actions. First, the free will of a man inclines him toward the good; it chooses the good.[24] Then it removes the obstacles and breaks the fetters which had kept him in sin, banishing from the heart *self-pity, man-pleasing, the inclination to the sensual,* and *earthliness.* Free will replaces them by awakening a pitilessness towards self and a distaste for the sensual, by inspiring him to subject himself to every kind of shame

---

23   Just as we are enjoined by the Savior to love perfectly, with all our power, so here Theophan enjoins us to hate that which is opposed to the spiritual life with all our power.

24   Prior to this, the man inclined himself toward the good by his will alone. Now by virtue of his ascetic labors, the man's freedom and free will naturally incline to the good. This is a significant advance along the way that leads to salvation.

and disgrace, and by resettling the heart in the world to come, implanting in it the feeling that we are strangers and pilgrims in this world. Finally, the free will of a man inspires him to enter the way of godliness and honesty, not indulging him at all, but keeping him in a certain constant tension.

In this way everything becomes quiet in the soul. A man who has been awakened by grace, having delivered himself from the captivity of all bonds and fetters, with perfect willingness says to himself, *Having risen up, I will go.*[25]

From this minute on, *another movement* of the soul begins— *the movement towards God.* Having overcome himself, having taken control of all the outlets of his own emotions, having restored freedom to himself, now a man must offer all of himself as a sacrifice to God. Consequently, for the present, the work is only half done.

---

25   Cf. Luke 15:18

12

Dedicating Oneself to God

One would think that everything was already finished if the decision to renounce sin has been made, and all one has to do is act. And indeed, one may act. But what sort of activity would this be, and of what spirit is it? For the time being, a man still dwells in himself alone. If he would begin to act starting from this point, then he would act following his own will and to his own advantage. Even though he would be acting morally, this would be an egoistic, selfish morality—pagan. There are people who say that they are doing good for good's sake; they do this because it is demanded by the moral dignity of man, or because it would be ignoble, dishonorable, and imprudent to act otherwise. These people show that the formation of the inward moral man[1] has not yet been accomplished in them. They have come to themselves,[2] but they have not forced themselves to advance from self to God and have not offered themselves to Him as a sacrifice. Consequently they have lingered at the halfway point.

The goal of the freedom of a man is not in itself and not in a man, but in God.[3] In freedom, God granted to a man, as it were, a certain portion of His divine authority. But He did this in order that a man, by himself and of his own free will, might voluntarily offer it as a sacrifice to God as the most perfect offering. That is why, if you have mastered yourself, you must go and dedicate yourself to God. When you were sinning, you were not only losing yourself, but you were estranging yourself from God as well. Now returning from sinful captivity, after you have mastered yourself, restore yourself to God.

---

1   Cf. Ephesians 3:16
2   Cf. Luke 15:17
3   Cf. John 8:31–35

One would think that turning from self to God should be an easy and simple matter, like, for example, turning from west to east. But a sinner who is drawing near to God is not a person who is independent from Him, and he does not approach Him in a way that suggests he has no obligation. No, he is the same as a runaway servant returning to his master; he is the same as a guilty one who appears before a king and judge. Therefore, he must draw near in such a way that God might receive him. According to human customs, a master receives his servant and a king grants pardon to the guilty one when each of them, drawing near, confesses his guilt, repents of it, and sincerely promises to be completely faithful in the future.

So also in the return of a sinner to God. He will be received by God if:

1. he acknowledges his sins,
2. he repents of them, and
3. he makes a vow to sin no more.

These are indispensable acts for the reunion with God in the heart. On these acts depend the firmness and steadfastness of the new life, the perfection of it, and the assurance of constantly acting in accordance with the requirements of this new life. The prodigal son, deciding to return to the father, said, *"I will arise and go to my father, and I will say to him, Father, I have sinned"*—the acknowledgment of sin; and *"I am no longer worthy"*—a repentance; *"treat me as one of your hired servants"*—the vow to work.[4]

KNOW AND ACKNOWLEDGE YOUR SINS

To return to God, you must *know and acknowledge your sins*. In the inspiration of your decision to renounce sin, you knew that you were sinful. Otherwise what would be the necessity of thinking about reforming your life? But at that time, this sinfulness seemed vague. Now you must find out precisely what was sinful and to what extent—clearly and separately. Get to know, as it were,

---

4   Luke 15:18, 19

the number of your sins, with every circumstance which diminishes or increases the sinfulness of your actions. Critically and thoroughly examine the whole of your life with a strict, impartial
judgment.

To do this, compare the law of God with your own life and
scrutinize in what ways they are similar and in what ways they are
not. Take your every deed and apply the law to it in order to see if
it is lawful; and take the law and see if it is being realized in your
life. In order not to miss anything in this important task, keep to
a certain order. Sit down and recall all your obligations in relation
to God,[5] to your neighbor,[6] and to yourself,[7] and then look back
over the whole of your life according to all these relations. Or
analyze the Decalogue[8] and the commandments of the Beatitudes,[9]
one after another, together with all their supplements,[10] and see if
your life is similar. Or read the chapters of the Gospel according
to St. Matthew in which the Savior expounds the Christian law;[11]
also the Epistle of St. James, the final chapters of the Epistles of St.
Paul the Apostle in which he briefly expounds the works which
are obligatory for a Christian—for example, from the twelfth chapter of the Epistle to the Romans, from the fourth chapter of the
Epistle to the Ephesians and so on. The final chapters of Ephesians
and Romans are especially important for the fact that they set
forth and elucidate the spirit of the Christian life. This spirit is
also expressed clearly and powerfully in the First Epistle of St.
John the Theologian. Read all this and compare your life to it, to
see if it is similar. Or, finally, take the Rite of Confession[12] and

---

5   Cf. Matthew 22:37, 38
6   Cf. Matthew 22:39, 40
7   Cf. Matthew 16:24–26
8   Exodus 20:1–17
9   Matthew 5:3–11; Luke 6:20–23
10   Cf. Matthew 5:13—7:29
11   Matthew 5—7
12   This refers to the penitential service book containing directions for confessors,
prayers, questions to be asked, and an exhaustive list of sins with an appropriate penance prescribed.

judge your behavior according to it. Review your life and your deeds not just as the deeds of a simple man, but as the deeds of a man who is Christian and besides, as one who has a certain calling and election.[13]

In consequence of such an examination of your life, there will be revealed a multitude of lawless actions, words, thoughts, feelings, and desires which should not have been, but you permitted them. A multitude of actions which you ought to have done, but you did not. And what is more, many of those deeds which have been done will turn out to be polluted and profaned because they were done out of impure motives. There will be gathered a great multitude of these, and perhaps even the whole of your life will prove to be fashioned from evil deeds alone. The main thing that you must bear in mind on this first degree of knowing your sinfulness is to discern with strict exactness your sinful deeds. As the service record of your deeds is being written with numerical precision, so also every man must conceive in his mind a list of his deeds with the same precision—with every circumstance of time, place, persons, obstacles and so on. If our self-examination remains fruitless, then this is because we are making only a general review.

In the presence of all this, however, you must not stop with these details, but you should go further along the path of sin and enter more deeply into the sinful heart. Beneath our actions, words, particular thoughts, desires, and feelings there lie the constant dispositions of the heart that constitute our characteristic traits. Some of our actions have burst forth by chance, whereas some have come straight out of the heart and with such intensity that there was no power to stop them. But some were done incessantly and have turned as it were into a law.[14] Such an examination will give us

13   Cf. 2 Peter 1:3–11
14   According to the teaching of the Church Fathers, all of the deeds, words, thoughts, desires, and feelings which have become a law for us have become our passions. Our passions now constitute a law for us, and rule us. Out of these passions, our sinful desires arise; cf. Galatians 5:16–24.

knowledge about *the producers* of each sinful deed,[15] which are concealed in the heart and which give birth to the constant impulse for doing these deeds.[16] Precisely these producers are our sinful inclinations. Uncovering them, we will reveal the nature of our heart—the number and mutual combination of its inclinations.

When this is done, the principal passion which governs everything will not be able to conceal itself as well as before. It is known that the root of every sin[17] is self-love. Out of self-love come pride, greed, and sensuality[18]—and out of these come all of the other passions, among which eight are considered to be the principal ones. And as for the rest, which are derivative, there is no number for them. Each sinner has all the passions—some are manifested in actions, others are in embryonic form—because every man who sins is governed by self-love, the seed of all passions and sinful inclinations.

But not everyone has them all manifested to the same extent; one is dominated by pride, another by sensuality, and a third by greed. The proud one is not alien to sensual pleasures, but he can do without them as well. And the greedy one also thinks highly of himself, but on occasion he would not mind stooping to a base act if it profits him. And the sensualist too is greedy, but it is all right if he suffers material loss when that loss is the cost of his pleasure. So every sinner has one principal passion. All the other passions are standing in its shadow and are governed by it, not daring to act with power contrary to the will of the principal passion. All evil inclinations and depraved habits, which have already been uncovered by a man within himself, are overshadowed by a single passion and inspired by it. This principal passion is the one in

---

15 That is, each passion.

16 Theophan is conveying a critically important set of ideas. The observable behaviors—deeds, feelings, thoughts, and so forth—are generated by the passions that are hidden in the heart. These passions must be observed and rooted out. It is not enough to try to control outward manifestations of the producers of sin. We must go to those inward parts concealed in the heart, which constantly produce a new harvest of sin.

17 In this passage, Theophan is using the words *sin* and *passion* as virtual synonyms.

18 This could also be rendered as *lust*.

which the root of all evil, self-love, is most present and realized. The full understanding of your sinfulness must be accomplished by *knowing* this principal passion.[19]

In this way, you will finally come to know the root of your sinfulness and its most immediate offspring, the inclinations, and the subsequent offspring, which are your numerous actions. You will see the whole chronicle of your sinfulness and you will depict it like a painting on a canvas.

STIR UP FEELINGS OF REPENTANCE

Having come to know your own sinfulness, do not remain its cold spectator, but strive to stir up *feelings of repentance of heart*[20] that correspond to your sinfulness. One would think that these feelings would arise within you by themselves as soon as you know sin, but in actual fact this is not always so. The heart grows hardened and coarse from sin. As a worker who does black work[21] becomes hardened and coarse, so also a man-sinner becomes hardened and coarse, by selling himself into the black slavery of sin—the slavery of digging up husks and feeding on them.[22] That is why you must work at perfecting yourself here as well, in order to stir up a feeling of repentance.

To come to these feelings of repentance, you must pass through the feeling of *guilt* on account of your sins and the impossibility of justifying yourself. The feeling of guilt stands between the knowledge of your sins and your feelings of repentance, and is itself brought about by your *self-condemnation.*

---

19   This *knowing* is not instantaneous or even quick. Rather, it is a long process of perceiving and understanding that is hard-won and difficult to achieve. It is the fruit of a long and disciplined examination and confession of one's sins.

20   These specific feelings of repentance are natural to the sinful heart, and are not something that has to be grafted onto one's nature.

21   Here Theophan plays on the meaning of *black*. Black work, in Russian, refers to unskilled labor like ditch-digging, which dirties and coarsens the laborer. He compares this black work with the labors of sin, which cover the soul with filth and make it hard and coarse.

22   Cf. Luke 15:11–32

Begin then, first of all, to condemn yourself—and condemn! Eliminate everything from your attention and leave yourself alone with your conscience before the face of God, the all-seeing Judge. Disclose that which you knew a man should not do—yet nevertheless you lusted after these things. Even in your lusting, you could have desisted from doing these things, but you did not make use of your power over yourself for your own benefit. Your understanding and conscience were against this, and there were obstacles[23] without, but you despised all these means of bringing you to your senses.

In the same way, do this with each of your sins. You will see that your every sin is committed willingly, with the full awareness of its sinfulness and, what is more, with an effort to overcome these obstacles. Your conscience will compel you to acknowledge your incontrovertible guilt. A deceit of the sinful heart will begin perhaps to invent excuses—now in an infirmity of your nature, now in the strength of your temperament, now in the coincidence of circumstances, now in the pressure of worldly relations. Do not listen. All these could intensify the inclination to sin, but no one can ever force you to assent to sin—it is always a matter of your free will. If you say, "No, I do not want it"—then all the temptations are over! Contrary to these *excuses for your wicked deeds,*[24] disclose more fully and thoroughly your own relations: what you are; where, when, and how you sinned—in order to reveal precisely the measure of sin in your person and in your circumstances. You will see in everything not reasons for excuses, but the things which magnify your guilt. You must bring the work of self-condemnation to the point where you feel an inexcusable guilt; the state in which your heart will say, "I have no justification—I am guilty."

In this act of condemnation by his conscience, a man will affirm one sin after another as his own, and will say, "I am

---

23 These obstacles are placed there by God to keep you from committing a sin.
24 Cf. John 15:22

guilty in that, and in another, and in a third . . . in everything, in everything." He will clothe himself in his sins and begin to experience that they lie upon him with all their heaviness. In knowing one's sins, one can still imagine them existing outside oneself; but in self-condemnation they are seen precisely within us and they press down with all their weight on our conscience. And they weigh upon us all the more because of the fact that we cannot justify ourselves in them. Having reached this point, what else remains for a sinner except to say, *"I am damned!* It is not that this was not right and that was wrong. I have to say that I alone am guilty and that these things are present within me."

As soon as a man will utter in his heart, *"I am damned,"* immediately the painful feelings of repentance for his sins will begin to revive in him, one after another. He *feels ashamed* that he has given himself over to such base actions. He *is annoyed* that he has indulged his passions and yielded to the persuasions of his wicked will. It *pains* him that he has reduced himself to such a state of moral disorder and enervation. He *is afraid* that he has insulted God and placed himself in a dangerous situation, both in time and in eternity. These feelings follow one after another and a man burns in them as in a fire. He sees himself as suspended over an abyss, and in his feelings he descends to the state of those who are outcasts, beyond salvation.[25] This inconsolable anguish makes a passageway to the feeling of hopelessness. And here is a point at which the demon of despair sometimes seizes a man-sinner, suggesting, *"Your transgression is so great that it will not be forgiven."*

Every sinner experiences these feelings to a greater or lesser extent. You must not regret that they exist, but rather should desire that they be more and more intense. The more a man burns in them and the more intense the burning, the more saving and beneficial the effect. In the intensity of this burning lies the foundation of

---

25   There is a remarkable similarity between St. Theophan's imagery and that of the Puritan preacher, Jonathan Edwards, in his sermon, "Sinners in the Hands of an Angry God," where he describes sinners as dangling over the abyss of hell suspended by a single thread, which is the grace of God.

future perfection. Here the heart learns from experience how bitter the fruits of sin are, and from this it draws the strength necessary to turn away from sin's charms.

CORRECT WHAT IS INCORRECT

Feelings of repentance obviously have a dividing effect. A word pierces, dividing asunder the soul and spirit, the joints and marrow, and discerns the thoughts and intents of the heart.[26] But the goal for which this is produced by God's grace within a man is not only to destroy, but through this destruction of the old, to create anew. That which is new is sown by the gentle breezes of hope for the possibility of amending everything. There is a possibility to correct what is incorrect and to recover what is lost; just set about the work and begin.

One would think that from these feelings of repentance there lies a straight way to the vow, "So I repudiate sin and make the promise to serve only God in the keeping of His commandments." The one who makes such a vow should be confident that, on the one hand, his former faults can be forgiven, and on the other, that he can receive strength for assistance in standing firm in his vow. That is why making a vow to serve the Lord is mediated by the assurance of pardon and the assurance of receiving succor from above. This assurance is produced by faith in the Lord and Savior, who tore up the record of our trespasses on the Cross[27] and, after His Ascension, *His divine power has granted to us all things that pertain to life and godliness.*[28] Without this faith, and without the assurance which is produced by faith, a man is pinned by crushing feelings of regret and follows the path of Judas.[29]

This is the very moment when the Cross of the Savior is indeed the anchor for a man! Being tossed as if over an abyss in painful contrition for his sins, he beholds the Cross of Christ as

---

26 Cf. Hebrews 4:12
27 Cf. Colossians 2:14
28 2 Peter 1:3
29 Cf. Matthew 27:3–5

his sole savior, catches at it with all the strength of his faith and hope, and from it derives strength of inspiration for making a vow. As a drowning man holds fast to a log, so also one who is repentant of his sins holds to the Cross of Christ and feels that from now on he may not perish. Usually we know the power of Christ's death on the Cross, but one who has passed through this painful repentance of his sins *experiences* it. From that time on, it becomes an integral component of his life.

So, pinned by the feelings of repentance, being shaken by a hopelessness, and advancing towards the long-wished-for vow:

1   First of all, hurry to revive your lively faith in the power of Christ's death on the Cross. All the sins of all people have been nailed to the Cross,[30] and yours as well. Quicken your trust in this certainty, and a gentle breeze of consolation and joy will blow into your heart. Assurance will arise in your heart immediately after it is warmed by this faith.

2   To this, add a firm confidence that the strength for keeping this vow will be given to you as soon as you draw near to partake of the Sacraments. There is no denial in them to anyone. They have been purchased by the Lord precisely so that they might be given to the faithful. This confidence will also stir up your own powers and bring forth the willingness to work hard in the presence of such succor. Will the vow arise without confidence of succor from above? On the other hand, will this confidence come if one does not think about the vow? This is a reciprocal interaction.

3   And so, when this combination of confidence and willingness takes place within you, make a vow to serve only God for the *remainder* of your life. This vow of the heart, which is sincerely given according to faith in our Lord Jesus Christ, will dispel all the darkness and gloom that had covered your soul, and will illumine all the threads of the interior life and all the planes of your outward life.

---

30   Cf. Colossians 2:13, 14

Here is made a covenant of the heart with God in Christ Jesus. Therefore, in this action your previous decision takes on a true Christian character.

13

Total Forgiveness Is Granted

The movement of a repentant sinner towards the Lord is accomplished by ascending to the vow to serve Him only. Now the penitent will merely take certain steps in order to receive the Lord, who is coming to meet him. The father met his prodigal son by embracing and kissing him as a sign of the total forgiveness of his transgressions. Then he put the best robe on his son, a ring on his hand, and sandals on his feet, and furnished a table for him.[1] Just as the father met his son, God pronounces the total forgiveness of his transgressions to the repentant sinner in the Sacrament of Confession. He clothes him with strength from above and offers him supper in the Sacrament of the Eucharist.

When a man-sinner has reached the point where he has made a vow to serve God alone from now on, he must hurry to the Sacrament of Confession. The indispensability of this is so great that everything which has been done until now will not only remain incomplete without it, but will also go for naught. The whole of its importance, all of its significance, and all of its strength is gained in this Sacrament alone. That is why, where there is no Sacrament of Confession, there are none who live a genuine Christian life.

1   The first reason that makes this Sacrament indispensable is a kind of instability in the inner spiritual work in general, some indeterminateness and unsteadiness about it. Our thoughts, while they are still in our head, are changeable and variable in their progression, inharmonious and disordered, and unsettled in their movement. This is the case not only when a subject is not comprehended or understood yet, but also when we have

---

1   Cf. Luke 15:20–23

discussed it thoroughly. But as soon as we have put our thoughts in writing, then they not only become settled in an order, but they are also finally comprehended and become firmly established.

In precisely the same way, the change of one's life, while it is conceived only within a person, is indecisive and not firm by itself; and these new forms of life which are outlined at this time are unsteady and indeterminate. These new forms assume a steadfast settledness in the Sacrament of Confession, when a sinner confesses his transgressions in the church and affirms his vow to be perfect.[2] Melted wax pools about indeterminately; but when it is poured into a mold or stamped with a seal, then some particular thing is made out of it. And to our inward man, one must affix a seal so that he might take a certain form and character. This is accomplished in the Sacrament of Confession; here the divine grace of the Spirit seals him.

2   A man receives spiritual life from the Spirit of God. The grace of the Spirit is mixed in with us. It begins to dwell and act within us and it brings forth life after the nature of the Spirit.[3] Prior to this, grace acted on a repentant sinner from without: it awakened and activated him from without, and from without it supervised all corrective and remedial movements and assisted them. But it had not yet penetrated within; it had not yet made its abode there.[4] This abiding is accomplished by grace in the Sacrament of Confession (but in one who has turned to the Lord for the first time, this is accomplished in the Sacrament of Baptism). As a man who is parched with thirst feels coolness and refreshment after a drink of cold water, so also a man who is burning with the fire of repentance receives in the Sacrament of Confession the power which finally soothes his afflictions and at the same time strengthens him.

3   And what particularly makes the Sacrament of Confession

2   Cf. Matthew 5:48
3   Cf. Romans 8:1–17
4   Cf. John 14:23

indispensable is, on the one hand, the nature of sin, and on the other, the characteristics of our conscience. When we sin, we think that the traces of sin do not remain, not only outside of us but also within our own selves. However, sin leaves deep traces both within us and outside of us, upon everything that surrounds us, and especially in heaven, in the determinations of divine justice. In the moment of sin it is determined in heaven what the man who committed the sin has become: in the Book of Life,[5] he has been inscribed on the list of those who are condemned, and has been bound in heaven. Divine grace cannot fall upon him until his name is blotted out in heaven from the list of condemned ones, until he has received absolution there. But God was pleased to make this heavenly release—this heavenly blotting out from the list of the condemned—dependent upon the release of those who are bound by sins on earth.[6] So, partake in the Sacrament of Confession that you might be considered worthy of a complete release, and so that you might clear an entrance for the Spirit of grace to come within you.

Our conscience—which has now been cleansed and purified again, and which has been restored to its natural tenderness and aptitude for moral order—will give us no rest until we become decisively convinced of our forgiveness. Such is the conscience in the usual course of our life; it does not allow us to appear in the presence of a man whom we have insulted until we have become convinced that he has forgiven us. But with respect to God, our conscience is even more exacting and delicate. When a man rises up to make a resolute vow to serve God, although a certain assurance falls upon him—that now he is not opposed or disgusting to God—this assurance is his own, so it cannot be steadfast or firm. Soon a doubt will shake it: "Is this really so? Maybe this is self-delusion?" and the doubt

5   Cf. Revelation 20:12
6   Cf. Matthew 18:18

will bring about an alarm and disturbance within, and from this disturbance, listlessness. In the presence of all these, life will have neither firmness nor harmony. So a man must hear the forgiveness of all his sins from God Himself in order that, finally having settled himself down by the assurance of God's favor and mercy, he might then act more resolutely and firmly in this certainty. Go then, confess your sins and you will receive the declaration of forgiveness from God.

GO NOW TO CONFESSION

One must properly prepare for this saving confession. A man who has accomplished everything that has been said above, that one is ready. Draw near then with reverent faith!

1   Having been firmly convinced of the necessity of this Sacrament, go to it. Go, not as to some auxiliary measure for changing your life, or as a simple, ordinary custom, but with full and absolute faith that for you, as a sinner, this is the only possible way to salvation. That leaving this out, you will remain among those who are condemned, and consequently outside all mercies. That having not entered into this hospital, you will not restore health to your spirit and will remain as you have been—sick and disordered. That you will not see the Kingdom if you will not enter it through the gates of repentance.[7]

2   By means of such convictions, revive within yourself the desire for this Sacrament. Draw near to it, not as to a place of slaughter or immolation, but as to the fountain of every good. He who vividly imagines the fruit which is brought forth within us by confession cannot help longing and striving for it. A man goes there with all his wounds. From the soles of his feet even to his head, there is no wholeness; there is nothing sound

7   To repent means to make a radical change in one's life as a whole. Both Jesus and St. John the Baptist began their public ministries with the same message. See Matthew 3:2 and 4:17. Theophan's point is that we return to Paradise through repentance.

in him, only bruises, welts, and raw wounds.[8] But he returns from there healthy, active, and strong in all his parts, with the feeling of safety from future contagions. He goes there under a heavy burden. The totality of his past sins lies upon him; it torments him and deprives him of all peace. But from there he returns lightened, having been relieved, and rejoicing in spirit that he has received the charter of forgiveness for all his sins.

3 Shame and fear will begin to cling to you—let them! This Sacrament should be desired precisely because it puts shame and fear in you; and the more you feel shame and fear, the more beneficial it will be for you. Desiring this Sacrament, desire to experience even more shame and to feel even more trembling. As for the man who is making up his mind to undergo treatment, does he not know about the painfulness of the treatment? Of course he knows. But deciding for treatment, he also destines himself for the sufferings which will attend it, in hope of recovery. And you too—when you were pining away in the painful feelings of repentance which had come upon you and when you were striving to draw near to God—did you not say, "I am ready to endure any suffering, just have mercy and forgive me!" And here your wish is being fulfilled. Do not let your heart be troubled with the shame and fear that are coming upon you. For the sake of your well-being they are linked with this Sacrament. Having gone through the fire of shame and fear, you will become morally stronger. You have already burned in the fire of repentance many times—burn a bit more. At first, you were burning solely before God and your conscience, but now burn a little in the presence of the witness[9] who has been appointed for this ministry by God, to testify to the sincerity of that lonely burning, and maybe, to complete its imperfection. There will be judgment, and there will be a desperate shame and fear with it. Shame and fear during confession expiate the shame and fear

8   Cf. Isaiah 1:6
9   That is, the priest who is receiving your confession for God.

of that time. If you do not want those, then overcome these.[10]

And besides, it always transpires that, according to the intensity of the disturbance through which the confessant goes, so also comforts and consolations abound in him after the confession. Here is the very place where the Savior truly manifests Himself as the Comforter of all those who labor and are heavy laden![11] A man who has sincerely repented and frankly confessed his sins knows this truth from the experience of his heart rather than by faith alone.

4   Then, having again recalled all the sins which you have committed, and having renewed the vow which has already matured in you not to repeat them any more, stir up in yourself the living faith that you stand before the Lord Himself who receives your confession, and tell everything, concealing nothing that burdens your conscience. If you have drawn near with the desire to put yourself to shame, then you will not shelter or conceal yourself, but you will depict as fully and completely as possible the ignominy of your eagerness to sin. This will serve for satisfying fully your broken and contrite heart. One must be confident that every sin which is confessed is vomited out of the heart. But every sin which is concealed remains in the heart to an even greater condemnation, because of the fact that the sinner with this wound was near the Physician who heals all the diseases of our souls and bodies.[12] Having concealed sin, he covered his wound, not regretting that the sin torments and disorders his soul. In the story about Blessed Theodora (Lives of the Saints, March 26), who after her death was passing through the aerial tollhouses,[13] it is said that her

---

10   If you do not want the shame and fear of the Last Judgment, then pass through the shame and fear that attend confession with a priest.

11   Cf. Matthew 11:28

12   Psalm 147:3; 103:3

13   It is sometimes taught in the Orthodox tradition that after death, the soul passes through some twenty aerial tollhouses where one's sins are brought forth in turn. For a further explanation of this concept, see Fr. Seraphim Rose, *The Soul After Death,* published by St. Herman of Alaska Press.

malicious accusers did not find in their scrolls those sins that she had confessed. Later on the Holy Angels explained to her that confession blots out sin from every place where it is registered. Neither in the Book of Conscience, nor in the Book of Life, nor in the scrolls of these wicked destroyers is this sin written down under the name of that person—confession has blotted out these entries.

So vomit out unreservedly and without concealing everything that is a burden to you. You should reveal your sins to the point that your spiritual father can form a clear and exact understanding of you. So that he might see you as you are, and loosing, he might loose precisely you and not some other person. That when he pronounces, "Forgive and loose this penitent from all the sins he has committed," nothing might be left within you that would not come under these words. Those do well who, preparing for confession for the first time after a long time dwelling in sin, find an opportunity to talk beforehand with their spiritual father and to recount to him the whole story of their sinful life. For these there is no danger of forgetting or missing something in the agitation and confusion that occur during confession. It is essential to take every care to make a full and complete revelation of your sins. The Lord gave power and authority to His ministers to loose sinners from their sins, not unconditionally, but upon the condition of their repentance and confession. If this is not fulfilled, then it might happen that when a spiritual father pronounces, "I forgive and release,"—the Lord will say, "But I condemn."

5 Here the confession is completed. The spiritual father raises his epitrachelion,[14] covers the head of the penitent with it and, keeping his right hand upon the epitrachelion, which covers the penitent's head, pronounces the prayer that absolves him from all his sins, sealing the absolution with the sign of the

---

14 The type of stole worn by the priest in the Orthodox Church. It is a long strip of silk, fastened in front and decorated with crosses and a fringe.

cross on his head. What happens at this moment in the soul is known to everyone who has frankly repented and confessed his sins.[15] Streams of grace pour from the head to the heart and fill it with comfort, consolation, and joy. This is not of men: neither of the penitent nor of the priest who absolves him. This is the mystery of the Lord, who is the Healer and Comforter of our souls.

In the presence of all this, it sometimes happens that a divine word is distinctly heard in the hearts of some for inspiring and strengthening them in their future labors. This is a spiritual weapon which is bestowed upon a man from Christ the Savior. Now he enters the company of those warriors who are ready and willing to fight under His banner.[16] Let a man who has been counted worthy to hear such a word keep it then, as a soothing, reassuring, and inspiring aid. It is soothing and reassuring, for the divine word makes it evident that the confession was received, since God was well-pleased to enter as though into conversation with the penitent. It is inspiring, because in the time of temptation he needs only to recall it and he will immediately feel a surge of inner strength. By what means do warriors inspire themselves during a battle? By means of that word spoken by the general of the army before battle which affected them most powerfully. So it is here also.

6   This makes everything complete. All that is left is to fall down before God with feelings of thanksgiving for His unspeakable and ineffable mercies, and to kiss the Holy Cross and the Holy Gospel[17] in token of the vow to follow the way of self-crucifixion[18] that is shown in the Gospel without deviation.

---

15   That is, told his sins to God in private confession in the presence of a priest who is appointed by the Lord for this ministry.

16   Christ's banner is His holy, precious, and life-giving Cross.

17   In the Orthodox tradition, the penitent, after receiving absolution, kisses the cross and the book of the Gospels in token of his resolve to lead a new life.

18   Cf. Romans 6:6; Galatians 2:20

All that is left is to follow Christ the Savior, coming under His easy yoke[19] which you have taken upon yourself only now. Having accomplished this, go in peace with the intention to act without fail in accordance with that which you have promised, keeping in mind that from this time on you will be judged by your own words.[20] If you make a vow, hold to it. If it is sealed by the Sacrament, be faithful to it all the more, so that you might not find yourself again with those who tread down grace.

7   If your spiritual father has imposed a penance[21] on you, accept it with gladness. But if he does not, then ask him for one. This will not only be a blessing for the good path on which you embark, but will also be a protection, safeguard, and cover from those foreign and inimical actions that are arrayed against you in this new order of life.

Here is what His Holiness, the Patriarch of Constantinople, writes in response to the Lutherans: "We accompany the remission of sins with penance for many good and valid reasons. *First,* so that a sinner, through voluntarily suffering afflictions *here,* might be delivered from a grievous and involuntary punishment *there* in eternal life; for there is nothing that so propitiates the Lord as suffering, and all the more, voluntary suffering. That is why St. Gregory says that one's tears are rewarded by God's lovingkindness. *Second,* in order to exterminate those passionate lusts of the flesh in a sinner which give birth to sin; for we know that an illness is healed by its opposite.[22] *Third,* so that a penance might serve as if it were a bridle for the soul and might not allow the soul to take up again the same depraved actions from which it is still cleansing and purifying itself. *Fourth,* in order to train a sinner to

---

19   Cf. Matthew 11:30
20   Cf. Matthew 12:37
21   Usually consisting of a certain course of prayer, fasting, and almsgiving.
22   For example, a high fever is treated by means of cold compresses. Penance is often called a "heavenly medicine," which heals the wounds inflicted by sin.

labor and to be patient, for virtue is a matter of labor. *Fifth,* so that we might see and know if a penitent has a true hatred for sin."[23]

He who goes through this course of spiritual treatment in the right way and, most importantly, confesses his sins without concealment, returns from the house of God as a guilty one returns from the court of justice, where, instead of receiving a death sentence, he has heard a declaration of pardon for his crimes. He returns with the deepest, most profound sense of thanksgiving towards the Savior of our souls. He has made a firm decision to dedicate the rest of his life to Him and to keep and do His commandments. He has a profound disgust for all his previous sins, and an eager desire to blot out every trace of his former sinful life. He who has been granted remission of sins feels within himself that he is not empty; he senses that a particular Power has visited him. Divine grace, which hitherto had acted on him only from without, now has entered within with the words of the priest, "I forgive and loose you from all your sins." Grace has become mixed with his spirit, and has filled him with a fervent desire and a quickening with which *he now goes forth to his work and to his labor until the evening of his life.*[24]

---

23 *Khristianskoye Ch'tenie (Christian Reading), Vol. 1,* 1842, p. 244.
24 Cf. Psalm 104:23

14

The Sacrament of the Holy Eucharist

In the parable of the prodigal son, the father, having received his son who came to him with repentance, after embracing him, kissed him as a token of forgiveness for all his sins. Then the father commanded his servants to bring forth the best robe and to put it on him, to put a ring on his hand and sandals on his feet, and to prepare a bright and merry supper.[1] The parental heart was not satisfied with the forgiveness he had granted; it wanted even more firmly to assure his son of his reconciliation with him, and to express more strongly the joy of meeting him after so grievous and painful a parting. Paternal love grants what filial hope did not even dare to expect. What sinner could expect something more after he had received remission of all his sins? But behold, he is nevertheless invited to partake of the Lord's Supper, where the Lord Himself gives him to eat His flesh and drink His blood.[2] This is the crown of bounteousness that is bestowed upon a sinner who is turning to a God-pleasing life. This is not something superfluous, but an indispensable and essential necessity in the work of reunion with the Lord.

The Christian life is life in the Lord Jesus Christ. A man who believes has put on the Lord Jesus Christ[3] and lives in Him and by Him. He who has fallen after baptism loses this grace. Rising from his fall and coming back to the Lord, he should again be counted worthy of it. And he is truly counted worthy through Holy Communion. The Lord says, *He who eats My flesh and drinks My blood dwells in Me, and I in him* (John 6:56). Here in the one who repents is the beginning of life in Christ Jesus. The Lord said that

---

1   Cf. Luke 15:20–23
2   Cf. John 6:52–56
3   Cf. Galatians 3:27; Romans 13:14

He is the vine and those who believe in Him are the branches
(John 15:4–6). As a branch cannot live by itself unless it abides in
the vine, so neither can believers unless they abide in the Lord.
There is no true life anywhere except in this vine. Everything that
is not in the vine is dead. That is why a man who wishes to live the
true life must be grafted into the vine, partake of its vital richness
and live, feeding on it. This grafting is accomplished in the Sacrament of the Eucharist; here a Christian becomes one with the
Lord. When the Lord was merely guiding a sinner to a full and
complete repentance, He was just knocking at the door of the
heart. But when the heart opens by means of contrition and repentance, He comes within and feasts with the partaker.[4]

Now a man is being born anew.[5] He begins a life which is of
an entirely different nature. This life cannot continue without
nourishment, and moreover, that kind of nourishment which is
natural for it. And this particular kind of food is precisely the
Body and the Blood of the Lord. He Himself said, *My flesh is food
indeed, and my blood is drink indeed* (John 6:55). A man who has
begun the new life must feed this life with precisely this sacra-
mental food. It is all the more necessary to partake of this food
during the initial stirrings of this new life. They say that a
person's first nourishment has an influence on the life of the
flesh, and afterwards constitutes a constant desire of the body.
What kind of life, then, must be in a man who has repented?
Life which is in Christ Jesus, our Lord. What must be his constant desire? The desire for communion with the Lord. Let him
hurry, then, at the initial stirrings of this life to partake of the
precious and holy Body and Blood of the Lord. This lays down
the foundation for a life that conforms to Christ and engenders a
vital and genuine desire for constant communion with Him by
means of partaking in the Eucharist. The partaker, having experienced the sweetness of this manna, afterwards cannot help

4   Cf. Revelation 3:20
5   In the Orthodox understanding of repentance, it is a process, not a once-for-all
event. This is never more clearly stated by St. Theophan than in this passage.

hungering and thirsting after this divine supper more and more.

So, having received pardon and forgiveness for all your sins in repentance, draw near to the Holy Eucharist for the full resuscitation of your inner man.

There is no need to prescribe any special rule to prepare for this. A man who has repented already has everything needful for this and he naturally proceeds to communion. He who mourned over his sins and confessed them is ready to partake of this great Sacrament. The Apostle does not prescribe anything more. He only says, *Let a man examine himself and so let him eat of that bread, and drink of that cup.*[6] One may say, "Keep what you have and do not lose what you possess; this is sufficient."

According to the rule that has been established in our Church, not much time passes between confession and communion; for the most part, there is only evening, morning, and then the Divine Liturgy. During this time one should take care to preserve the favorable inward disposition which has been brought from church after confession, and to apply it to communion with the Lord in the Holy Eucharist.

1   Keep your attention undistracted and your heart undisturbed. Guard yourself from distraction and from the agitation of worldly cares. Having laid aside everything of this kind, enter within yourself and abide there with the thought of the Lord alone, who is about to come to you. Eliminate every movement of your thought and, contemplating the Lord alone, pray to Him with the undistracted prayer of your heart.

2   If your thought cannot abide in this one thing, then give it the exercise of reflecting upon the Eucharist itself; and so that it might not wander, bind it by the words of the Lord and those of the Holy Apostles about this Sacrament.[7]

3   Reflecting upon some sentence of the Lord or the Holy Apostles, derive edification from it and dispose yourself to

---

6   1 Corinthians 11:28
7   Matthew 26:26–28; 1 Corinthians 11:23–30

contrite prayer. When the prayer comes, fall down before the Lord and do not depart from the prayer until it works within you.[8]

4 Spend the evening in these exercises until sleep closes your eyes. The morning will come. As soon as you come to yourself, upon awakening, first and foremost bring to mind the greatness of this day for you. But do not fret, do not be distracted with many things. Keep your mind on this alone: what is about to happen to you and within you. Take heed, be watchful and sober! The enemy will tempt you in every way possible in order to put your soul into a state of confusion, trying his best either to distract your thoughts, to engender worries about something, to ignite dissatisfaction over something, or to rouse your resentment against someone. Be on guard for yourself; pray to the Lord, and you will escape these stumbling blocks.

5 Having come into the church, feel as if you were in the upper room in Zion where the Lord gave communion to the Holy Apostles, and harken to what is being chanted and read, directing everything to the thought that this is the Lord Himself who prepares for you the Supper that brings salvation.

6 Stir into flame your *faith* in the actual presence of the Lord Himself in the Holy Sacrament. Relying upon this faith and contemplating the Lord Himself, who is already coming to you, call to the Lord in *self-abasement, "I am not worthy to have you come under my roof."*[9] From self-abasement, proceed to filial *fear*, which does not separate you from the Lord, but brings you to a reverent and pious sobriety.[10] Inasmuch as the Lord Himself invites and commands you to draw near, be ready to partake *in all confidence,* with *desire* and *thirst*, as the deer

---

8   When this prayer operates in an individual, it is important not to leave it, but rather to stay with it and allow the grace of the Holy Spirit to work secretly in the heart.

9   Matthew 8:8

10   Spiritual sobriety refers to the attainment of dispassion, the state of having overcome one's passions of pride, greed, and lust by means of the spiritual disciplines and inward prayer.

pants for the water brooks, and in the sure and certain *hope* of receiving the Lord Himself, and with Him all the treasures of life which are hidden in Him. From this earnest longing and hope, which will not put you to shame, turn again to yourself with a willingness to meet the Lord. Stir more vigorously into flame the *contrition* of your heart, and renew your *promise* to turn away from sin, even if you must die for it.

7   During the Divine Liturgy, exert yourself to stay with these feelings, passing from one to another. Finally, in this well-favored inward disposition, draw near to the cup of the Lord, and having beheld it, give worship to the Lord who is coming to you. And having opened your lips and your heart, receive Him; having cried unto Him humbly and reverently together with the Apostle Thomas, *My Lord and my God!* [11]

Glory be to Thee, O God! Glory be to Thee, O God! Glory be to Thee, O God! [12] Having drawn near to the cup of the Lord with such an inward disposition and stepping back from it, you will feel in your heart: *It is truly said, that having communed of divine grace, I am no longer alone but with Thee, my Christ, the three-sunned Light that enlightens the world.* [13] Henceforth, you begin to bear Christ within you. Take fervent care, then, to guard Him in every possible way and to retain Him within yourself. If Christ is within you, who can be against you? And you will be able to do all things through Christ the Lord, who strengthens you. [14]

This completes the work of forming the spiritual life within a Christian who, after falling into sin, again converts to a God-pleasing life.

---

11   John 20:28
12   This is a quotation from the Prayers of Thanksgiving after the Holy Communion from the Divine Liturgy.
13   This quotation from Slavonic is taken from the prayer of St. Simeon the New Theologian that is recited during the preparation for Holy Communion.
14   Cf. Philippians 4:13

This is the whole order of conversion! It is described here in the form of a long narrative in order that he who is turning to God might see more clearly all the turns that he must make, as man's freedom and God's grace interact. Every man who turns from sin to a God-pleasing life passes through all these turns; but how and to what extent—this depends on the person and the circumstances. One can have the whole matter of conversion accomplished in a few minutes, during which he passes through a grace-given awakening, a repentance, and then ascends to the decision to renounce sin and devote his life to God. Spiritual phenomena are instantaneous. However, examples of this kind of conversion are very rare. For the most part the whole matter is accomplished not at once, but gradually. Although the inner changes themselves are instantaneous, one does not always reach them quickly, but sometimes only after a rather long labor of self-perfection. That is why, for some, complete conversion takes years.

The chief points on which one lingers or delays are those where one's self-love must suffer: for example, at the time when it is necessary to overcome the obstacles on one's way to salvation, to overcome the inciters of sin, at the time of the confession of one's sins, and so on. The final state that one must reach is the complete and total separation from everything, so that nothing possesses one, and the commending of oneself to the Lord. Precisely from this minute on, the full and genuine Christian life begins, because at this time a man has reached his goal—and now his life is hidden with Christ in God.[15] Everything depends on the initial zeal with which one begins this work of self-perfection, and on one's conviction of the fact that what is necessary must be done. Whether now or later, it must be done, and better now. When he starts working, he soon settles into his way. And getting settled is the main purpose of conversion.

---

15 Cf. Colossians 3:3

Index

A

affliction 27, 92, 112, 119
Andrew, Blessed, Fool-for-Christ 20, 21
angels 20, 22, 57, 87, 115, 126
anxiety 6, 61
appetite 25
Art of Prayer, The ix, xxxiii
ascetic labors xvi, xvii, xxxii, xxxvi, 71
asceticism xix, xxiii, xxix, xxxiii
assent to sin 105

B

Baptism, Sacrament of 1, 3, 58, 112, 121
Basil, Elder xv, xvi
body 26, 36, 49, 50, 59, 79, 95, 122
Body of Christ 58, 122

C

catechism 35, 64
Christ 1, 11, 14, 18, 21, 22, 33, 37, 53, 57, 59, 61, 69, 87, 107, 108, 118, 121, 122, 125, 126
Christian law 54, 101
Church xix, xxxii–xxxiv, 18, 21, 29, 30, 35, 38, 51, 68, 69, 112, 123, 124
    Russian Orthodox xv, xviii, xxv, xxx, xxxvi
Church Fathers ix, xvi, xix, xxiv, xxxii, xxxiii
confession of thoughts xvii
Confession, Sacrament of 1, 11, 12, 51, 68, 111–115, 117, 118, 123, 126
conscience 2, 24, 57, 59, 74, 77, 91, 105, 113, 115, 116
contemplation 22, 29, 31, 79
conversion 11, 12, 14, 20–22, 24, 29–31, 33, 38, 42–44, 63, 64, 79, 126
creation 29, 30, 35, 36, 76
cross
    sign of 118
    way of 18
Cross of Christ 37, 59, 107, 108

127

D

death 21, 27, 32, 34, 36, 57, 59, 60, 66, 69, 108, 116, 120
  of St. Theophan xxxiv, xxxv
delusion 22, 32, 46, 52, 72, 113
demons 9, 33, 106
desire
  evil 6, 102
  for God 2, 5, 14, 43, 45, 64, 81, 84–86, 114, 120, 124
devil 25, 32, 59, 66, 87. *See also* Satan
dissatisfaction 23, 76, 124
divine order 18, 19, 21, 22, 36, 37, 78
Dostoevsky, Fyodor xiii
dreams 20

E

Eucharist, Sacrament of 11, 12, 111, 121–123
evil 2, 3, 36, 42, 54–56, 59, 69, 74, 86, 88, 89, 95–97, 102, 103
  life 44, 49
  one 33

F

faith 1, 5, 33, 35, 53, 64, 107, 108, 114, 116, 124
fall into sin 1, 24, 59, 83, 84, 121
Fall, the 8, 53, 92
fasting 49, 51
fear 2, 13, 19, 26, 28, 32, 34, 42, 74, 75, 115, 124
  of God 31, 55
flesh 3, 8, 26, 27, 46, 49–51, 71, 92, 119
Florovsky, Georges xiii, xxv
free will 3, 81, 84, 86, 97, 99, 105
freedom 3, 4, 9, 23, 24, 27, 37, 42, 61, 81, 94, 96–99, 126

G

greed 90, 103

H

habit 44, 83, 103
heart xxix, xxxi, 1–3, 6, 7, 9, 10, 13, 15, 18, 19, 24, 38, 41, 45,
  46, 49, 51, 52, 55–60, 65–67, 70, 71, 74, 76, 78, 81, 84, 86,

O

Optina elders xvii–xix

P

passions 9, 26, 34, 76, 90, 103, 106
Path of Salvation, The ix, xix, xxxiii
patience 69, 120
  of God 58, 59, 66
Paul the Apostle, Saint 20, 34, 36, 43, 101
Peter the Great xv
Philokalia, The xvi, xxxiii
podvig 30
prayer xxix, xxxi, xxxii, 67, 68, 70, 71, 85, 89, 93, 94, 117, 123, 124
pride 103
priest 35, 118, 120
procrastination 44, 45, 60, 71
prodigal son 11, 32, 37, 100, 111, 121

R

reason 33, 42, 44, 59, 63–65, 67, 68, 71, 85, 86, 94, 95
repentance 1–3, 5, 11, 31, 33, 36, 51, 100, 104, 106–108, 111,
    112, 115–117, 121–123, 126

S

Sacrament. *See* Eucharist, Sacrament of; Confession, Sacrament of
Satan 8–10, 32–34, 87. *See also* devil
self-humiliation 89
self-indulgence 7, 8, 25–27, 32
self-love 103, 104, 126
self-perfection 79, 82, 126
self-pity 90–92, 95, 97
sensuality 75, 90–92, 103
Seraphim of Sarov, Saint xvi
shame 31, 33, 46, 74, 77, 89, 91, 97, 115, 116, 125
sin 1–4, 7, 8, 10–14, 33, 35, 38, 44, 46, 51, 56–60, 66, 70, 73,
    74, 80–82, 86–88, 92, 95–97, 99, 100, 102, 104, 105, 107,
    113, 116, 119, 125, 126
  coverings of 49
  inciters of 89, 91, 92, 94, 96, 126
  supports of 96

Introductory books on the Orthodox Church:

*Note: prices listed were current as of January, 2001. Prices are subject to change. When ordering directly from publishers, please enclose additional funds to cover tax and postage & handling.

THE ORTHODOX CHURCH

By Bishop Kallistos Ware (Published by Penguin) $14.95

This classic introductory work on the Orthodox Church has become a worldwide standard in colleges and seminaries. Part One describes the history of the Orthodox Church. Part Two outlines Orthodox doctrine and worship. The final chapter deals with restoring the breaches between East and West.

INTRODUCING THE ORTHODOX CHURCH

By Father Anthony Coniaris (Published by Light & Life) $14.95

Fr. Coniaris provides his readers with an invaluable introduction to the beliefs, practices, and patterns of Orthodox Christianity. Written in a popular and easy-to-read style, *Introducing the Orthodox Church* touches all the important bases without sacrificing balance or accuracy.

THE ORTHODOX FAITH (4 volumes)

By Father Thomas Hopko (Published by Orthodox Christian Publ. Center) $29.95 set

An introductory handbook on Orthodox faith and life. Volume 1: Doctrine/ Volume 2: Worship/ Volume 3: Bible and Church History/ Volume 4: Spirituality. Presented in brief chapters, this handbook series is excellent for quick reference or study, and provides valuable teaching material for both teens and adults.

DIVINE ENERGY

by Fr. Jon E. Braun (Published by Conciliar Press) $9.95

Applies time-tested Orthodox spirituality to contemporary Christian living. A true "back to the basics" book which shows how Christians can fight and win the struggle against temptation, sin, and spiritual lethargy through the divine power of Christ's Incarnation.

THE ORTHODOX WAY

By Bishop Kallistos Ware (Published by St. Vladimir's Seminary Press) $10.95

An excellent companion to *The Orthodox Church*, this book discusses the spiritual life of the Christian, and sets forth the basic issues of theology, but as a way of life for the follower of Christ.

THE APOSTOLIC FATHERS

Edited by Father Jack N. Sparks (Published by Light & Life) $12.95

Contains modern translations with introductions of the writings of early Christian Fathers such as Clement, Ignatius of Antioch, and Polycarp. These revered writings helped launch the Evangelical Orthodox Church on its journey to Orthodoxy.

APOSTOLIC SUCCESSION

by Fr. Gregory Rogers (Published by Conciliar Press) $3.95

Examines the unbroken apostolic chain linking past to present in the historic Church. Written by a former evangelical pastor whose study of the biblical and historical evidence supporting this very doctrine led him to chrismation and finally ordination in the two-thousand-year-old Orthodox Church.

BECOMING ORTHODOX

by Fr. Peter Gillquist (Published by Conciliar Press) $12.95

The inspiring story of over two thousand evangelical Christians and their search for historic Christianity. This book is for evangelical Christians on their own search for the Church. It is also for Orthodox Christians looking for renewal.

To request a Conciliar Press catalog, place a credit card order, or to obtain current ordering information, please **call Conciliar Press at (800) 967-7377 or (831) 336-5118, or log on to our website: www.conciliarpress.com**